STRUGGLE

TED EVANS

DISCLAIMER

In this book, I have tried to recreate events and conversations from my memories of them. Some names have been changed to protect the privacy of individuals.

FOREWORD

If you have ever had the privilege of working on an occasional project, participated in a sports event, or an athletic season, or perhaps taken a trip with Ted, then you learned rather quickly that Ted has goals and a strategic plan to achieve those goals.

Now Ted has undertaken another project: writing a book. A most important endeavor. As Ted has interacted with people (primarily college-age students), he has seen a yearning by many young people to find answers in the quest for a relationship with God. As Ted weaves questions and answers regarding this incredible process, he's invited a number of people—Ted's plan—to join with him in sharing their thoughts on this most important of relationships.

Ted bares his soul about the struggles in his life in hopes that, as you read these stories, both humorous and gripping, your relationship with God will be ignited or strengthened.

Sincerely,
MATT AND JOHN NAFIE

INTRODUCTION

My name is John Evans, but since pre-school I have been known by my middle name, Ted.

I am a retired teacher and coach of forty-six years, at the high school and college level in both public and Christian schools.

During my career, I coached a men's fastpitch team for seventeen years, three college women's fastpitch teams for sixteen years, and an acrobatic team known as America's Anti-Drug Acrobatic Team for ten years.

In my family I am the middle son, three years younger than my brother Clyde, and eleven months older than my brother Tim. As Tim and I were so close in age, people often thought we were twins.

Tim and I were in the same grade and we went to public school together through the first eight grades. We were crazy about sports. As we got older it became more and more difficult for us to balance our feelings about athletics versus the philosophy of the Seventh-day Adventist (SDA) church of which we were members. The church took a strong stand against athletics in the fifties and sixties.

Clyde liked to play tennis (our family sport), but otherwise wasn't particularly interested in sports. He never went to public schools, instead attending SDA schools, and was always a model Christian. I struggled to understand why this was so easy for him and so hard for me. He wasn't an easy brother to be measured against.

My dad was an elder in the SDA church, heavily involved in church activities, and a natural born leader. He was also a teacher and coach in the public school that Tim and I attended. The kids he taught and coached loved him, and his teams won many championships. He was also my coach during much of my early life. I loved my dad; he was my hero!

My mom was a musician who played the piano and the organ. As well, she gave piano lessons and my brothers and I were required to take lessons from her. I liked piano lessons about as much as she liked playing tackle football. Clyde was the only one who liked playing the piano. Mom was a rigid, uncompromising, and legalistic SDA. At our house, she was the boss. You did it her way, no discussion. To make matters worse, she wasn't fond of sports. I'm sure she meant well, but it didn't set well with me from early on.

Growing up in a strict SDA home, the denominational doctrines of the SDA church were first and foremost, and they were enforced in a legalistic way. Many of those doctrines were about things that we *could not* do. We could not go out on Friday night; we could not ride bikes or play games on Saturday; and we could not dance, play cards, read comics, or go to the movies. We didn't eat meat or consume caffeine drinks like Coke and coffee. If you smoked or consumed alcoholic beverages, you could not join the church. Organized sports were banned in SDA schools.

My Christian experience was like a roller coaster ride for most of my life. At an early age I struggled with Christianity. I would make a Christian commitment and later show no semblance of being a Christian. Most of the time, after a Christian commitment, there would be a conflict with sports and the doctrines of the SDA—and I almost always chose sports. I struggled with why there were such strict prohibitive restrictions on what I could do compared to what my non-SDA friends could do. I wondered why God gave me athletic talents but my church didn't allow me to use them?

It seems ironic however, that the SDA doctrines I had been taught permeated my soul and, while I may not have always practiced them, I continued to at least think about them. As an example: When I played professional baseball, I would keep my batting average on Friday night and Saturday separate from the other days to see if they were different.

During my professional career as a teacher and coach, I discovered that many young people from various denominations experienced the same Christian struggle that I had. Many abandoned their earlier Christian life for various reasons. One being that the religious teachings in their home were dominated by denominational doctrines instead of a focus on Jesus Christ. I believe that this is one of the foremost reasons many young people, of all denominations, leave their churches. I know it was a major factor for me.

Growing up in this world as a Christian can be difficult. Many great temptations make it hard to live a consistent Christian life. Some seem to be able to overcome these with ease, while others, like me, found a Christian life to be a real struggle.

If this sounds like you, do not give up. There is hope. A consistent Christian life is available to all with God's help.

It is my hope that through my experiences and the testimony of other Christians, you will find strength, inspiration, and keys to living the Christian life you desire.

Sincerely,
TED EVANS

WHY SUCH A STRUGGLE

❦

The Reverend Billy Graham had just finished his impassioned spiritual presentation. Twenty thousand people were packed into the football stadium to hear the great evangelist, including me and my family. I was probably seven or eight at the time. Dr. Graham finished his presentation with an invitation for anyone who would like to make a commitment to the Lord to come down to the stage in the middle of the field. George Beverly Shea began singing "How Great Thou Art" and Clyde immediately sprung to his feet and began bounding down the steps.

I was really unnerved as Clyde disappeared into the huge crowd.

"Dad," I screamed, "we'll never find Clyde!"

"He'll be fine," he answered.

And indeed, he was.

Clyde would say years later that this was a defining moment in his life. He knew there was a God, and even though he didn't know what his life's calling would be, he knew it would be in some way helping his fellow man as part of God's plan.

Clyde was bullied at an early age and yet he seemed to be able to take it, walk away, and hold no animosity. He was in so many ways a model child and a model Christian. He was a straight-A student, and he was responsible beyond his years. He virtually never got into trouble. Clyde and I were very different and these differences manifested themselves at a very early age. I hated being compared to him.

I often wondered why it was so easy for Clyde to be a Christian. I thought it was amazing how he maintained such a steadfast relationship with the Lord. He was kind, gentle, and caring. He pursued ways to help others. He didn't need to be the center of attention, but had the unique ability to be supportive of those who were. He had a great and contagious laugh and those telling a joke loved having him around. He was willing to give advice when asked, as God had given him the unique ability to make so many feel fulfilled just by being a good listener. I took advantage of this trait later, especially when my troubled life took some difficult turns and I needed his advice. Clyde was always there!

While Clyde had the Lord as the center of his life, I had sports. It was my driving force from a very early age. It soon became evident that I was pretty good at various sports, including baseball, boxing, basketball, football, tennis, and track and field.

Willie Mays, the great San Francisco Giants centerfielder, was my childhood hero. Because of this, there was no doubt in my mind that I was going to be a professional baseball player.

Unlike Clyde, I was bullied very little because when and if it happened, there was going to be a fight. Unlike Clyde, my grades were not great, however I did make straight A's in PE! I was having a lot of fun and didn't think a lot about God. And I was constantly getting into trouble, especially at home.

Tim and I were in the same grade. Many thought we were twins, but we were actually born in the same year nearly eleven months apart. I was born on January 1st and Tim on November 23rd. We were very close and both loved sports.

While we were in the same grade, it didn't start out that way. I didn't go to kindergarten. I don't know why, but when I went to first grade Tim went to kindergarten at the same school. On the first day of school, Tim walked into my first-grade room and sat with me. My teacher, Ms. J, came to my desk and asked Tim to go back to his classroom.

Tim just sat there and mumbled, "I want to stay with Teddy."

Ms. J asked him several times to return to his room but he refused to leave, always giving the same response. She finally got frustrated and grabbed him roughly by the arm. I jumped up and slugged her in the stomach. She immediately grabbed me and marched both of us to the principal's office.

I remember thinking that I was going to jail. Our parents were called, and when they got there both of our teachers, the principal, and my parents decided that Tim was advanced enough to attend first grade and be in the same classroom with me. I guess it is understandable that it would not be in Ms. J's room.

I think this was the first time that I can remember being Tim's protector. I was always bigger than Tim and felt it was part of my responsibility to help protect him. The other kids knew that when you messed with Tim you messed with me.

Our first organized sports experience was in the Pee Wee Baseball League. That summer I was eight and Tim was seven, and we desperately wanted to play in the league. My parents were split on whether we should play, and in the end it was decided we should not. We were heartbroken. We would ride our bicycles to the games and dream about playing in the league.

One night about a month into the season, Mr. Logan, the league commissioner, came to our house and talked to our parents. He explained that one of the coaches was transferring out of town and his son was the pitcher. Their team was in last place and needed a lot of help. Mr. Logan was pleading with my dad to take over the coaching of the team and to bring Tim and me with him. If dad refused, the team would be dismantled.

My mother was never very excited about sports, but after a few days of holding our breath, my dad told us that they had decided we were going to play the second half of the season.

My dad was a great coach and loved by the kids. He immediately held practices, and when the second half started, we were ready to go and it was really exciting.

Tim and I were the pitchers for our team. I threw harder than Tim but he had better control. Tim seldom walked a batter. I on the other hand, walked some and hit some. Most of the kids couldn't hit when I was pitching, probably because they were scared. I was having the time of my life!

I ended up leading the league in batting average and home runs. We were undefeated and won the second half of the season. This gave us the right to play for the championship against the team that won the first half. The first half winners were good, but we had beaten them in the second half and were confident going into the championship game. Final score: 8 to 7. We lost. I learned something about myself that day; I hated to lose. Tim and I cried.

WHY CAN'T WE JUST GET ALONG?

Mom never attended any of our baseball games. I think it was her way of showing her objection to our involvement. This was my first recollection of any serious dissension between us. She was uncompromising about her views, especially those about SDA beliefs.

Mom was definitely in charge, and she was moody. When she was unhappy it was very evident by the look on her face. Fortunately, most of the time she didn't stay unhappy for long. We all knew that when you saw "the look", as we called it, you had better keep quiet and stay out of her way. We all had our own way of dealing with her; dad would go to his shop, Clyde would go for a walk, and Tim would go to his room and keep quiet.

As for me, mom and I had a very strained relationship, especially for the first twenty years of my life. I refused to give in to her. My defiance was constantly getting me into trouble. I was strong willed and hated to be bullied by her, especially without at least having some discussion. When mom had "the look", I stayed and voiced my opinion.

People told me I looked like my mom and (before puberty) even sounded like her. I would answer the phone and mimic her perfectly.

One day my teacher called and I answered, sounding just like mom, and got an update on how Teddy was messing up. I told my teacher I would handle it. Unfortunately, mom talked to my teacher a short time later and I was busted. Oh well, it was fun at the time and worth it.

Dad told me on numerous occasions that the problem between me and mom was that we were just alike. I didn't believe this and I hated the thought of it. How could I be like her?

What made things even worse was how different Clyde and I were. As the older brother he was the standard bearer. Clyde was soft-spoken and always respectful. He never quarreled with anybody, and was never involved in a fight. I on the other hand was loud, a ruffian, and defiant. I wore many of Clyde's hand-me-downs as they were still like new, but I wore them out so fast it became a constant frustration to mom.

Two things that really drove mom crazy; I wet the bed and chewed my fingernails.

I wet the bed until I was around twelve. This became a real source of frustration for both of us. I had been taught that God hears and answers our prayers, so each night I would pray that I wouldn't wet the bed. And each time I did, I would wake up and ask the Lord to help me quit. I would try to sleep on one side of the wet spot, but I mostly lay awake brooding about the chastising that was sure to come in the morning. My family nicknamed me "Pee Body", or "Wet The Bed Ted". It was a constant nightmare. I often asked God: Where are you, why don't you help me?

One day when I was about nine, I got into a fight. My parents were really upset with me.

"Why did you get in a fight?" Mom asked.

"Because he called me a nasty name," I said.

"Remember, if someone calls you a name, that's what *they* are." she said.

That night I wet the bed, and the next morning mom called me "Pee body".

I responded: "Well then, that's what *you* are."

I received a slap across the face that I can still feel to this day.

That night I ran away from home. I didn't go far, in fact just to the back yard. When my folks discovered I was gone, there was hysteria. I know, because I was hiding right outside the room where my mom was and watched her crying. I felt jubilant and triumphant, and that I had won. Later my dad let our dog out and she found me in about thirty seconds.

Chewing my fingernails was the other issue. I didn't know why then, and still don't. Between the ages of about nine to thirteen, a variety of punishments were levied if I didn't stop biting my nails. Dates were scheduled for fingernail inspections and when I failed, and I always did, it was no dessert, or no attendance at a particular activity. Since that had little effect, they decided I should receive a spanking if I failed. You would have thought that would work, especially as a prayer preceded the spanking; but it didn't.

One Christmas I had asked for a motorized airplane that flew on the end of control lines. You wouldn't believe how elated I was when I got the exact one I wanted. I sat on the floor admiring it. WOW! It was bright red and beautiful.

"Let me see it," Mom said.

I handed it to her.

She stood up and said, "You can play with it when you stop biting your nails."

I sat there in disbelief; but this also had no effect.

A few months later she decided to give me the plane and I followed her to its hiding place above the water heater. When she pulled it down, the plane's plastic wings had melted from the heat. It was ruined! I stood there staring at it for a moment, then walked off before I gave her the satisfaction of seeing me cry. There was no mention of maybe getting another one.

I continued to bite my nails until I was twenty-four years old, only quitting when I decided I wanted to quit.

As I grew older I realized that many of my problems with mom were my fault. I knew how to "push her buttons". I saw her as a "bully" and I refused to give in to her. The great news is that thanks to the

7

goodness of God, and the willingness of us both to try, mom and I became quite close later in life.

I must point out that mom did have a soft side. One time after I had gotten into trouble she told me to go to my room. I knew I was going to get a whipping, so before she came in I slid pieces of cardboard into my jeans. When she hit me with the belt I didn't react, and after the second or third strike she realized something was wrong.

"What is going on?" she asked.

I pulled the cardboard out of my jeans and she laughed hysterically. She was still laughing as she walked out of the room, and without delivering another strike. It was the best whipping I ever had.

In our home, mom insisted that we should always be busy. Idle hands were the devil's workshop, you know. Sports were not an appropriate way of staying busy in mom's eyes. This was a constant source of frustration with Tim and me. If there was nothing else to do, we were required to pull weeds from the lawn.

One day, when Clyde was home from school, we were in the back yard pulling weeds. Actually, we were doing more talking than weed pulling. Suddenly mom opened up a window and told us to get to work.

"We're on break," I said.

"Get to work or you don't eat," was the reply.

Of course, I couldn't help but pull her chain and said, "If we don't eat, we don't go to church."

She slammed the window and came running out of the back door swinging a broom at me. She chased me around the back yard while Tim and Clyde laughed hysterically. She finally gave up, but she was not happy.

Clyde would always defend mom; "Remember, she and dad were both orphans and did not have homes to model."

It was true; mom and dad were both orphans.

Dr. Johnstone and his wife, who owned a large ranch in Hanford, California, took in a number of homeless kids. Mom was lucky enough to be one of them. She was seven at the time. Dad on the other hand was not so lucky and was pretty much on his own. He worked for farmers in the Hanford area who would give him a place to sleep and eat in exchange for his labor.

When dad was a teenager, he went to work for Dr. Johnstone. He had become skilled at fixing things, especially anything motorized. The doctor needed someone like him and told dad that if he would continue to work for him he would not only give him room and board, but pay for his schooling at the SDA school in the nearby town of Armona.

This of course was great in my dad's mind, especially since mom lived there as well. Dad had a crush on her the moment he saw her. She claims she didn't like him, at least at first. Mom and dad got married after their freshman year in college. As it turned out, Dr. Johnstone helped pay for dad's schooling all the way through college.

The rest, they say, is history!

LET THE ACTIVITIES BEGIN

&

*W*hen I was eight, dad started the Pathfinder Club at our church. Pathfinders are the SDA version of the scouts. The only problem for me was that you had to be ten years old to join. Becoming ten couldn't come soon enough.

The Pathfinder Club met every Tuesday night and they had crafts, marches, and various outdoor contests, such as making a fire using just flint and steel. A host of different badges could be earned to wear on your honors sash.

We lived in the San Joaquin Valley near Fresno. During the summer, the Pathfinders would often go to Sequoia National Park where it was 30 degrees cooler. We played a variety of search games and had teams where we practiced our skills while working on attaining our badges. At night the grownups would tell us stories around a large open fire. When the fire had burned down to a bed of glowing embers, we would roast marshmallows and make s'mores.

On Saturday night the big event was playing a game we called "Spy". All the kids were divided into two teams, each having twenty-five or thirty members and an adult leader. Team One was given a head start and had to stay together and within the prescribed boundaries. Team Two waited for ten minutes and then left camp to try to capture (find) the other team. The second team also had to stay together, except for one person who acted as the spy. The spy was sent ahead to locate Team One. If and when the spy saw the other team, he reported their location back to his team. The spy wasn't allowed to capture the hunted players; this was the job of his team. After Team One had been found, the two teams would trade places and the game would start again.

At the end of the night there were lots of wild tales about how close the pursuing team had come. It was part of the strategy to be perfectly quiet, and in the darkness it was common for the pursuing team to walk within a few feet of their opponents. On one such occasion, the pursuers had just passed by my team when one of our group, who had fallen asleep, began snoring. We were captured!

Another day we were playing a glorified game of team hide-and-seek. The team chosen to hide could split up into groups of three or more and hide within the designated boundaries.

Tim, our friend Danny, and I teamed up and decided to hide in an old barn. In one corner was a pile of rubbish that we moved so we could hide behind it. We settled in and stayed as quiet as we could.

Suddenly I felt something strange on my leg. I stood up and whatever it was crawled up my pant leg. If I didn't move, it didn't move, but as soon as I moved, it would crawl farther up my pant leg.

"Tim there is some creature that has just crawled up into my pant leg and every time I move it crawls farther up," I said.

"Whoa! That's not good!" Tim replied.

I was totally horrified and told Tim to go get dad.

While I waited, I suddenly became a serious Christian.

"Please Lord, do not let this varmint bite me!" I prayed.

Dad wasn't far away but it seemed like forever before he finally arrived. He told me to slowly undo my jeans and let them slide to the ground. When they were about halfway to the floor, a rat jumped out and scurried away.

I thanked the Lord for hearing my prayer.

In public school through the eighth grade, Tim and I played sports at school and in summer leagues.

We also joined a self-defense class. We started with Judo, which would improve our body awareness and balance. Judo was fun and challenging for a while, but after a year or so, we decided to pursue wrestling and boxing.

Tim really liked wrestling and excelled at it. I liked boxing, and the more I boxed the more I loved it. Being hit was never fun, but it was part of the thrill and challenge to hit and not be hit in return.

Growing up in the fifties, there were a lot of opportunities to fight, whether at the boxing club or on the street. While most kids shied away from physical altercations, there were still plenty who didn't. At the boxing club I gained a reputation for being a pretty good fighter, and most of the other kids my size wouldn't fight me.

My reputation spread onto the streets and some of the bigger, older kids would challenge me. These were scary moments. Fighting on the street had no rules and I had to learn to walk away.

It's been said that fighting doesn't accomplish anything: probably said by someone who had never been in a fight. I learned a lot about myself during those years and grew from my experiences. One of the best things boxing taught me was to always maintain control of your emotions. Unfortunately for me, this trait didn't always carry over to other sports or life experiences.

Clyde often wondered what kind of Christian growth could ever be gained from fighting. I would say to Clyde; I know all of my opponents, and most of the time we are actually good friends. At the boxing club, good sportsmanship was a strict requirement. At the end of each fight we would shake hands and congratulate each other.

"Didn't I act like a Christian?" I asked Clyde after a fight.

"Maybe, but I just can't imagine beating up somebody and calling it Christian," Clyde replied.

Clyde did get me thinking about this apparent conflict.

Tim and I stopped wrestling and boxing after our freshman year in high school. While it was mom and dad who ended our involvement, we were ready to make the change as we had become enthralled with baseball and tennis.

Another exciting activity was locating mom's and dad's siblings and their families.

One of the first we found was mom's oldest brother, Sam.

Sam and his family lived in San Leandro near Oakland. It was really exciting to be able to find and visit our real cousins: Ann, Nancy, Vince, and Sammy.

Over the next ten to twelve years we were able to find all of my parents' siblings. It was amazing to discover that two of mom's brothers lived within thirty miles of our hometown.

We never became really close to any of our cousins, except for Sam's children. We would sometimes stay overnight with them and go to the Giants baseball games at Candlestick Park. A few times, Tim and I stayed a week or so. On these occasions, all of us cousins would ride the bus into San Francisco and then down to Candlestick, where we could sit in the bleachers for fifty cents. Sometimes, when the security man got to know us, we were let in for free. Those days were great fun; and of course, I got to see my childhood idol, Willie Mays.

One day we arrived at the ballpark early, which we loved to do so that we could try to catch a baseball hit during batting practice. This day the Giants were playing the Pittsburg Pirates. The big slugger on the Pittsburg team was Willie Stargell.

When he came up for batting practice we all ran over to right field, as he was left-handed. It wasn't long before a long fly ball came right at me. I jumped and it hit off my glove and bounced between the bleacher seats. I dove for the ball and a bunch of kids jumped on top of me. I could hear Tim yelling, "Hold on Ted, hold on!" I was holding on for all my life and eventually I came out of the dog pile with the ball. For several years that was a cherished souvenir, even though it wouldn't have compared to a ball caught off the bat of Willie Mays.

Cousins Ann and Vince are still very special to me today. Ann and I are almost the same age. Tim and I loved her because no matter how much we teased her, she would give it right back. Vince is about three or four years younger, and he is also a lot of fun. The older he gets the more he resembles his dad, our favorite uncle. Cousin Nancy moved to Australia in 1970, when she was twenty. I haven't seen or talked to her since we were kids. She said she was going for six months but ended up staying. She may have planned to stay all along, but she couldn't tell her father; he would have had a cow. I also think she met a nice man and fell in love.

Unfortunately, Sammy was killed on Father's Day 2009 when the truck he was working on fell off the jacks. He was always known for being meticulously careful, so it came as a real shock. He was just forty-nine.

In the summer of 2017, Ann received a new kidney after an eleven year wait. Her health has improved dramatically and we are all thrilled for her.

THE INTRUDER

There was one time in my life that I thought I was going to die. This experience had a great impact on Tim and me, and our Christian experience.

After we graduated from eighth grade, our family went on a vacation to Lake of the Woods in Oregon with the Wonderly family.

The Wonderlys had two girls, Janet and Nancy, who were Clyde's age, and two boys, Don and Dick, who were Tim's and my age. Our two families owned a boat together. We had been on this same vacation before, but this year we had rented a newly built cabin and a separate old bunkhouse to be used solely by us boys.

This was going to be the vacation of a lifetime—water skiing, tennis, scuba diving, and some independence in the old bunkhouse.

Clyde had just graduated from high school and was heading for college. As the adult in the bunkhouse, he was charged with keeping an eye on the younger foursome. But Clyde didn't hang out with us, as he really enjoyed spending his time with Janet and Nancy.

We hatched a few plans to remind Clyde that we were still there.

The bunkhouse had three rooms. The first was a living room area with a massive old couch, an old dining table, and a small kitchen.

There were some metal plates and silverware that we washed ourselves and then placed on the table to dry.

The next room was to the right of the living room and it had two metal cots near the door with skimpy mattresses to lay our sleeping bags on. Dick and I slept on those. Clyde chose another cot that was against the far wall at the end of the room.

The last room was adjacent to the kitchen area. It had a great big old bed where Tim and Don slept.

On the first night in the bunkhouse, Clyde immediately went to bed while we four younger boys lingered around waiting for him to go to sleep. That didn't take long.

We decided to put to the test something we had heard about. We carefully put shaving cream in Clyde's hand and then tickled his nose with a feather. It worked! He raised his hand and wiped his face with the shaving cream. We screamed with laughter, but Clyde was not amused and told us to go have our fun elsewhere and let him sleep.

During the day, life at the lake was unbelievable, with numerous activities and lots of good food. But at night it was always fun to come up with some prank to play on Clyde. He continued to be unamused but that didn't deter us.

One night we fixed his cot so that it would collapse when he sat on it. It worked perfectly.

Another night, we put his hand in warm water. We had heard that this would make him wet the bed. Unfortunately, that didn't work.

He would always growl at us and act mad but we knew, as good-natured as he was, he kind of enjoyed it.

I must admit that Clyde handled this and most situations with Christian poise and restraint.

One night after we had all settled in our beds, I heard Tim whisper from the other room: "Ted, do you hear something outside?"

I listened and did hear something scratching around outside. This wasn't unusual as there was a lot of wildlife around, especially deer.

"I'm sure they will go away shortly," I tried reassuring Tim.

I was trying to be brave, but I was actually very concerned; I hadn't heard anything like this any other night.

It didn't take long for the sounds outside to stop, and I felt a lot better. It was quiet for a while but for some reason I couldn't sleep.

Then all of a sudden, BANG!

The outside door flew open and boom, boom, boom, boom. The old bunkhouse floor was vibrating with hideously loud thumping. Whatever it was started our metal plates and silverware around the room. It was pitch black; I couldn't see a thing.

"Look between the crack in the door and see what you see," I whispered to Dick, whose cot was behind our door.

Dick moved to look, but when his bed creaked the intruder bounded out of the bunkhouse.

Tim and Don ran into our room and slammed the door shut, quickly pushing our beds up against it.

To our amazement, Clyde was still sleeping peacefully. We ran over and began shaking him. He raised up and we were all shouting about the monster that had just been in the front room. Of course, Clyde was trying to figure out what prank we were pulling this night.

Then, BANG, the outside door flew open again and boom, boom, boom, the floor began shaking. We ran to our door and began to push against it. We listened to what we guessed was a bear, moving around the room upending the chairs. Every step it took made the bunkhouse shudder. It stomped across the room and suddenly —silence.

What was happening?

BOOM.

There was a violent thud as the couch was dropped, and the bunkhouse shook like never before. Can you believe it, that thing had picked up that huge couch?

We were praying fervently and committing ourselves to the Lord forever and ever. Clyde meanwhile was still sitting on his bed as if he wasn't going to fall for our latest gag.

Then the bear began scratching on the wall, working its way toward our bedroom door. Clyde bolted to the door as the bear tried to push it open, and we all pushed as hard as we could against this evil force. Finally the bear moved on.

We were sitting ducks; we couldn't get out of the bunkhouse because the bear was between the only exit and us.

We decided to open the window and scream for help. I volunteered to be the one to do the yelling. We had another quick session of prayer and then I opened the window, hoping there were no other bears outside.

I yelled as I had never yelled before.

Soon Mrs. Wonderly yelled back from the main cabin, "What's going on, boys?"

"Don't come over here there's a bear or some kind of monster in here. Call the police or fire department," I yelled back.

Mrs. Wonderly came anyway.

By this time, the bear had made its way into Tim and Don's room. Mrs. Wonderly walked into the bunkhouse and was walking toward the back bedroom, where the bear sounded as if it was on the bed.

We decided we must grab Mrs. Wonderly and sprint out of the bunkhouse.

We pushed the beds back, opened the door, and saw Mrs. Wonderly walking into Tim and Don's room. We ran in and grabbed her, and as we did, we looked to our left. To our amazement, on the bed, were the two Wonderly girls, Nancy and Janet.

They had staged the whole thing and later said that they thought we were playing along, but we were actually scared out of our minds.

We were so traumatized that we slept on the floor in the main cabin for the rest of the vacation. Clyde, however, showing that he was brave, slept by himself in the bunkhouse.

That experience was especially significant for Tim. He had made a commitment to God and he was going to keep it! From that time on and for the rest of his life, he read his Bible almost every day.

For me, this began an eight- or nine-year roller coaster ride with my Christian experience. I didn't want to be a Christian at that time, but I admired Tim for his dedication to his commitment.

TRANSFERRING TO CHRISTIAN SCHOOL

im and I were very competitive. We competed in everything we did, including ping-pong, badminton, tennis, and even who could do their paper route the fastest. It was amazing fun having a brother so close in age.

At an early age, we would pray before our games. One day, Tim and I prayed before a game of ping-pong in the garage. After that game ended, we prayed again. When we opened our eyes, dad was standing there.

"What are you doing?" he asked.

"We are praying that the Lord will help us win the next game," I replied.

"Hmm," Dad said, "Do you think God cares who wins, and don't you think you are putting the Lord in a tough spot when you are both praying for victory?"

He had a point.

From the age of seven or eight, Tim and I were involved in summer league baseball and tennis. We were fairly even in most sports, but Tim was the more finessed player while I depended more on speed and power.

As tennis was a favorite pastime in our family, and Clyde's favorite sport, we often played as a family. Tim and Clyde would play against dad and me.

Tim would always try to tell Clyde how to play and where to position himself, and in spite of Tim's coaching, Clyde would quietly do his own thing. After all, he was the older brother.

Dad and I would always say to each other: "There they go, they should be disintegrating at any time now."

Sure enough, Tim would get frustrated with Clyde and they soon fell apart, allowing dad and I to win.

After the game, Tim and Clyde would not talk to each other for several hours—a scenario that has replayed throughout our entire lives.

Tim and I continued to play both baseball and tennis every summer until after our freshman year in high school. That summer mom and dad decided we could not play both sports and we had to decide which one to continue with.

Tim chose tennis and I chose baseball.

That summer I won my last tennis tournament. After the match I saw a college coach talking to my dad. I couldn't wait to talk to dad after he left.

"What did the coach say?" I asked.

"He wondered what your interest would be in playing in college." replied Dad.

"What did you tell him?"

"I told him you wouldn't be interested because baseball was your first love. I also told him that your serve and volley were better than most kids your age but your groundstrokes were just average and you didn't love the game enough to fix it. Was I wrong?" he asked.

I knew he wasn't but I was not happy.

"Did you tell him we were SDAs?" I asked.

"Yes." said Dad.

This of course would mean I couldn't play on Friday nights or Saturdays, and no college coach would accept that.

This was the first time I began to question why the Lord would give me a talent for sports when I couldn't use it because of my religious affiliation.

After we graduated from the eighth grade, Tim and I enrolled at the local SDA school. This was something we hated because all of our close friends were going to the public high school and continuing to play sports. The church school had no athletics teams, and while this seemed to be no big deal to the kids at the Christian school, it was a huge adjustment for Tim and me.

The church school had classes from first grade through tenth grade. We liked the principal/head teacher and most of the kids, however we really missed the sports we had become accustomed to in public school. The principal was sympathetic to our situation and allowed us to play basketball in the gym after school.

It was interesting that Tim and I had always been challenged by our dad to make the public school our Christian mission field. We both accepted that challenge. We were very careful with our language, actions, and the jokes we told. We were especially careful when we competed: to be good sports, play fair, and congratulate our opponents.

You can imagine our surprise when we attended the church school —the dirty jokes that were told and the bad language that was commonplace. Bullying was also a common practice—the bigger, cooler kids were just plain mean to the smaller kids. I soon let my standards drop, as much as anything to at least to be accepted. After all, these were all SDA Christians who didn't need our help!?

Tim on the other hand, stood strong. I was actually proud and envious of his Christian resolve as he came under an array of peer indignation.

One day after school, two boys cornered Tim in the gym. When I walked in they were pushing him around and calling him names. They quit when they saw me.

"Our beef is not with you it's with Tim," one of them said.

"If you have a beef with Tim, you have a beef with me," I countered. I was really upset.

"Which one of you wants to fight with Tim? We will go up on the mats and you can wrestle until someone says give," I added.

I knew Tim could have killed either one of them with his wrestling skills, but they both declined and walked away. On their way out, I called them some ugly names. Tim wasn't too happy with me and felt that it could have been taken care of in a more Christian manner.

Later, we all became good friends and the next two years actually went quite well. We adapted to the games played at recess and played our preferred sports after school and during the summer.

SUMMER CAMP

I only went to summer camp one year. The truth be known, I was afraid to go because I was afraid I would wet the bed; and since we slept in a sleeping bag it could turn into a really embarrassing situation. I had pretty much stopped wetting the bed by the time I was twelve, especially if I didn't have a drink after supper, so that summer at camp went well from a wet-the-bed perspective.

On an overnight hiking trip to the top of El Capitan in Yosemite National Park, our campsite was about a hundred yards from the edge of a vertical drop. Tim had at times walked in his sleep and I was scared that he could become disoriented and walk over the edge. That night I prayed to God to protect Tim and to keep me from falling asleep so that I could keep an eye on him. I stayed awake and Tim slept like a baby.

That week we had a pretty good time, but crafts, campfire stories, and hiking were no match for tennis and baseball, which we could have been doing back home.

At the end of summer camp, I was glad that I had not gone to previous camps.

Three years later, in the summer of 1963, the camp director called and talked to mom. They were desperate for junior camp counselors and wondered if Clyde or dad would be able to assist for a week. Mom told him that both Clyde and dad were busy, but that I was available. I was fifteen.

"Could he be here early Sunday morning," the director asked.

"Let me talk to him, and I will call you back," Mom replied.

I agreed to go. It would be better than working in the fields. I asked dad what I should know about being a counselor. Among other things, I would be expected to lead in cabin worship.

"That's scary," I said.

"Why don't you dissect the Lord's Prayer and get the boys' ideas," Dad suggested.

"Yes, that sounds good," I said.

President Kennedy was to be at the Yosemite Valley on the Sunday afternoon and I thought it would really be neat to see him. Unfortunately, my ride was late and by the time I got to camp the buses to see the president had left. When the boys returned, they were introduced to me. They seemed like a nice group of kids, aged between ten and twelve.

They were very excited about a bear that had come into camp just before they had left to see the president. Some of the counselors said that this bear visited on a regular basis and it wasn't a big deal. Some of the boys in my cabin were a little freaked out by the experience, but at the same time hoped the bear would return.

That night we had our first cabin worship and started with "Our Father which art in heaven, hallowed be thy name". I was really surprised by how the boys jumped in and gave their perspectives on just those few words. By the end of the week I felt I had gained more from the exercise than they had.

The next morning reveille was played over the loud speakers and woke the camp. The camp director gave a few instructions and we were soon having breakfast in the cafeteria. After breakfast we were dismissed in cabin order and went outside to dump our garbage in the large dumpster, and then go through the wash line and wash our trays and silverware.

Then back to our cabin to make beds and tidy up. Each cabin was graded daily and awards given for the cleanest and neatest.

The boys in my cabin were excited for the day's activities, including games, crafts, and short hikes. But first, we all met in the center of camp for a general-rule meeting and announcements.

My cabin would be doing crafts first, and the boys were given a choice of what they wanted to make. The overwhelming choice was the snake catchers. I was amazed that they all wanted to catch a rattlesnake with their new toy.

After the morning craft session, we went back to the cafeteria for lunch. The boys were abuzz about the snake catchers they had made.

After lunch we were dismissed to go through the wash line, but we couldn't get to the dumpster. There, half in and half out, was the big grizzly bear.

Everybody was gathering around to watch, and no one seemed concerned. Occasionally the bear would raise his head and look around at us. He was hideous looking with his face covered in garbage.

Suddenly, one of the boys from another cabin ran up and hit the bear on the tail. The bear stood up tall and roared. I wanted to get out of there quick, but the bear just turned and went back to eating. The boy was given a stern scolding by his counselor.

I was wondering why we all just stood around with this huge wild animal within about fifteen to twenty feet of us.

Then it happened!

The same boy ran up and hit the bear on the tail again. The bear roared, jumped off the dumpster, and headed straight for another boy who was standing near the wash line.

The boy froze. The bear rushed up and stopped a few inches in front of him. He was growling in a low, menacing manner as he stared at the boy. He stood there for what seemed like an eternity.

I remember praying, "Oh, God, save this kid", even though I didn't think he had a chance.

Then the bear slowly backed away, turned, and ran out of the camp, with twenty or thirty kids running after him. Are you kidding? I couldn't believe it.

The next day the bear came back.

We (the counselors) had been instructed to assemble our groups inside the cabins or the cafeteria if the bear were to return. We all did exactly that.

The forest rangers were called and they shot the bear with a tranquilizer gun, relocating him an hour away.

BOARDING SCHOOL MISCHIEF

*I*n our junior year, Tim and I transferred to the Monterey Bay Academy (MBA), a boarding school on the Pacific Coast.

The school didn't believe in any kind of sports program, not even intramurals. We found this to be very frustrating and other less than honorable activities soon became part our time fillers.

One evening we were walking around campus and low and behold, there was a fire engine with the key in the ignition. There were even fire helmets that were the perfect fit. We decided to take it for a spin around campus, waving at everyone as we passed. The fun ended when two men caught up with us. They were big, mad and loud. Because we were all new students, the vice principal gave us a scolding and that was it. We left his office feeling like it was worth it.

Another time, we organized a football game on the front lawn. This was about as taboo as the fire engine ride. Some of us new guys challenged some of the returners. We were in the lead when the Dean arrived and stopped the game. He was quite upset and reminded us that these types of games were totally against the rules.

Tim had a longtime friend (Mack) from our hometown. He and I had fought many times. He was tough, but not really that skilled. He could take a punch like no else I had fought, but as long as he could get in some punches, he was happy.

I learned that he had pulled a dirty trick on Tim. I went down to his room and knocked on his door. There were several of his buddies in the room. I asked him to come out into the hall, but he refused.

"If you have something to say, say it," he said.

I voiced my displeasure with him about what he had done to Tim and told him I would make things right.

"You want to do something about it? Let's go right here, right now," he replied.

I knew better than to get suckered into this with all his friends around, so I said: "I'll meet you in the lobby in fifteen minutes."

I rounded up some of my buddies and he brought his, and we agreed on a few rules. I had a set of boxing gloves but he refused to use them. I believed he thought this was going to be to his advantage and I knew I had to be careful, especially in the early stages.

Mack did exactly as I thought he would and came out swinging wildly. He was strong and landed punches to my arms and body, but most of the time I was able to tie him up. Boxing and street fighting are tremendously exhausting and he soon became tired. I popped him with a few jabs and then caught him with an upper cut to the gut and he went down. He said it was a low blow but we both knew it was fair. He chose not to continue.

As a result, we were both called into the Dean's office and given a letter of admonishment. When we got up to leave the Dean asked me to stay, and then ripped into me. He was really angry. He told me I needed to clean up my act or I would be looking for a new school.

I really hated this place. Luckily some of my friends were here and so it was tolerable.

Mack and I later talked things through. He and Tim had made up and he wanted to be my friend as well.

At MBA, everyone had to work. Freshmen and juniors worked in the morning and went to school in the afternoon. I worked at the Mill, the furniture factory associated with the school. A bus took us to and from the factory each day.

One day before I left for work, Mack told me that this big kid, Sal, was talking it around that he was going to kick my behind. Mack thought it might happen that day. I didn't even know Sal, but one of the perils of fighting is that you become a target for those who want to make a name for themselves; a common pastime in the sixties.

Sal also worked at the Mill so I stayed vigilant. On the bus ride back to school, Sal was sitting in the front; he never did that. When we arrived, Sal hopped off the bus and headed up the steps. I started up the steps to my room on the second floor when, all of a sudden, I was tackled by Sal. He was big but slow and inexperienced. I soon had him in a chokehold and his friends were screaming for me to quit. I let him go and silently thanked Tim for letting me be his wrestling practice partner. Sal and I were both called into the Dean's office where we were given a letter of admonishment. Sal immediately said that it was totally his fault. I later told Sal that I respected him for doing that.

About a week later Ms. B, the cafeteria manager, asked me if I would like to work for her. I said that I absolutely would. Clyde had worked for her when he attended the school. She told me to be there Monday morning at 7:45 sharp. On Monday I was there around 7:50. She told me I was late, and that 7:45 means 7:45.

The next morning I had a stomachache and was late again.

When I arrived she said, in a very stern voice: "You're not like Clyde!"

"Thank you," I responded.

She got right up in my face and said in her most intimidating voice: "That was not a compliment! Do you want to work here or not?"

"Yes, ma'am I do." I thought I should stand at attention and salute. Clyde always set a high standard and I decided that I was going to win Ms. B over and be as good a worker as he was. I was never late for the rest of the year and in the end, really liked the job.

POISON OAK

*E*ach year, the boys club went to "Big Sur", a beautiful camping area along the Pacific Coast.

This particular year, several of us decided to tie seaweed together and stretch it between two trees on either side of the road.

The seaweed was about two feet above ground level. We had barely tied the seaweed when along came a Corvette, moving at high speed. The driver saw us running, and then the seaweed. He slammed on his brakes and slid broadside into and through the seaweed. He jumped out of his car and began chasing us up the hill. He didn't catch us, but when we returned to camp we saw the Corvette, and the man was talking to our school sponsors.

As a result of our prank and running through the brush, Tim got a serious case of poison oak. Covered from head to toe, he looked like something out of a horror movie. The doctor gave him a shot of cortisone to help relieve the itching.

A couple of days later, in the middle of the night, Tim's roommate came to my room and told me that Tim was acting really strange. We agreed to swap rooms for the night.

When I went to his room, Tim was on his knees praying and crying. He was pleading and begging that God forgive him.

"Tim, what's wrong?" I asked.

He told me that he had read in the Bible that we should love the Lord more than anything else, including our parents and brothers. I don't love the Lord that much. I tried to reason with Tim but he was distraught and spent the rest of the night moaning and praying. At one point, he said he didn't want to live. I could not believe what I was seeing and hearing. Tim was acting bizarre and I had no idea what to do.

The following morning, I called mom and dad with a report on Tim. They said they could come in a couple of days and to keep them informed. Until then I needed to stay close to Tim, so I talked to the dorm administrator.

The next day we went to church and that afternoon visited the rest home to spend some time with the elderly. Tim usually enjoyed reading to one of the patients, but this day he had no interest. I didn't want to bug Tim while we were there, but I wasn't going to let him get too far from my sight. I had no idea what he might do. All of sudden Tim started walking toward the wall that was between the rest home and the cliff overlooking the beach. As Tim climbed up on the wall, I ran up and grabbed him. He screamed at me and told me to get away from him.

When we got back to campus I called my parents again and pleaded with them to come and get Tim.

They left home immediately and were at the school three hours later. Seeing Tim leave with them was one of the saddest moments of my life.

At home, Tim was diagnosed with having a bad reaction to the cortisone shots he had been given for the poison oak.

He continued to act strangely. For instance, he had always been afraid of the dark, but now he was walking around our small town in the middle of the night.

After a couple of weeks, Tim returned to his old self; but he didn't want to return to MBA. This was disappointing for me, we had always been together, but I just wanted him to be all right. Tim started going to the SDA day school, Armona Academy, about thirty miles from home. After the holiday season, I tried to convince Tim to come back to MBA with me, but the negative experience was too much. He chose to stay home.

After the holidays, trouble just seemed to follow me. I'd picked the wrong crowd, although their mothers were sure I was the "wrong crowd."

One Saturday night, five of us skipped the program at the auditorium. MBA was formerly an army base, and we broke into one of the old barracks and took old army jackets, boots, and other attire. We walked around campus sporting our new duds. Then someone picked up a rock and threw it through a window. I don't know how it escalated, but soon we were throwing lots of rocks at lots of windows.

When it was over we all made a pact of secrecy. Do not tell anyone, anything. Needless to say, the windows were the hot topic around campus. About a week later the five of us were called into the principal's office and we were suspended for two weeks. They were, however, going to let us work with the maintenance department to replace the windows, paying for just the glass and materials. When the windows were replaced, we could all go back to class.

Right after this meeting, the dorm administrator called me in and told me I was no longer wanted at MBA. There was no doubt this man hated me. As I look back now, I don't blame him.

I did not appeal the Dean's decision. As soon as we had all of the windows replaced I went back home and attended Armona Academy with Tim.

CRAZY SIX WEEKS

J was quite nervous on my first day at Armona Academy. It was great being reunited with Tim but I was afraid my problems at MBA would be held against me.

The first order of the day was a worship assembly for the whole school. Afterwards, Tim came rushing up to me.

"Ted, come with me, I'm in trouble," Tim said anxiously.

We went to the men's room and Tim explained that he was to be sent home for wearing jeans. Jeans are not allowed and you are given one warning; he had already had his one warning. As I was wearing the appropriate slacks, he said we had to trade pants.

Tim was about five inches shorter than me at the time, so my slacks on Tim were dragging on the floor. Tim's jeans, now being worn by me, were about six inches above my shoes.

We walked into the principal's office and when he looked up and saw us, he cracked up.

"Ted," he said, "you are wearing jeans. They are not allowed. This is your first warning. If it happens again you will be sent home."

"Yes, sir," I said, being the totally respectful person that I am.

Neither of us wore jeans to school again.

My first class was with the other juniors, and it was wild. The teacher hadn't arrived and while we waited the students were throwing pencils, trying to stick them in the ceiling, and also shooting spit wads through straws at each other.

These kids are really rowdy, I remember thinking. Later that day we were playing basketball and a teacher came in and asked for the ball. The student with the ball, Kenny, refused to give it to him, and the teacher started chasing him around the gym. Before he could catch him, Kenny passed the ball to another kid, but the teacher grabbed Kenny anyway and began roughing him up. He eventually got him in a chokehold. I rushed over and screamed at the teacher to let him go. The teacher asked if I wanted some.

"No," I said, "but you have no right to rough him up like that."

The teacher walked out and strangely enough, I never heard anything else about it.

I couldn't believe all the chaos that first day. Many of the students were very disrespectful to the faculty.

In an effort to fit in, a few days later I "accidently" pulled the fire alarm. I was busted immediately and received a week's suspension. I spent the next five days in the library writing a research paper on fire prevention.

The librarian was Mrs. Qualley. She was the mom of Ron and Duane, two of my favorite fellow students. We did a lot of talking that week. Much of it was about my future and the importance of Christ in my life. I could tell that she really cared. She was really sweet, and I enjoyed my suspension.

A weekend or so later I really wanted to go to MBA for a visit. Tim was all in on the idea. Sunday morning came and we asked our parents if we could borrow the car. We didn't tell them that we were going to MBA, about three hours away, but we did leave them a note telling them where we had gone.

We got into the VW and headed out. We worried that dad would come after us. When we got to MBA we were greeted by the local police. They were actually quite nice, but informed us that we were not to leave campus until further directions were received from our parents. We agreed.

The next morning, we really wanted to go home but the police said to stay put, so we did. That was a long day as we really didn't know what was happening at home, and why we were just sitting and waiting. At 7:00 p.m., the police arrived and told us we needed to go home—straight home! We did just that.

When we walked into our house around 11:00 p.m., mom and dad told us to go to our rooms. I went to my room, undressed, and got into bed. They walked in a few minutes later.

Mom gave me some life-changing options.

"Ted, you have three options, you can go to Armona Academy and then go to work after school. Dad has found you a place of employment. The money you earn will be paid to us to pay for your room and board.

"Or you can go to Dinuba High School and go to work after school in a place dad has found that will hire you. The money you make will be paid to us to pay for your room and board.

"Or, if you don't like either of those options, then you are not welcome in our home."

I got up and got dressed without saying a word. I packed a few things and walked out, got on my bike, and rode the five miles to my friend Kenny's house.

I knocked on Kenny's bedroom window and he let me in. The next morning, I talked to Kenny's mom about staying with them. They lived on a farm and had a workers' room attached to the barn. At that time, they didn't have anyone staying there so she said I could. I agreed to work for them to help pay for my room and board.

Kenny was a junior at Armona Academy so I was able to ride to school with him.

At Armona things were not exactly going well.

About a week after leaving home, the students in each class voted for the person they wanted to act as the teacher for each class on student/teacher day. To my amazement, I was voted to be the industrial arts teacher. This was the same teacher that had roughed up Kenny.

When student-teacher day arrived, the industrial arts teacher didn't show up for the class.

"Today students, for our industrial arts class," I began, and after a pause shouted, "*we are going to play basketball!*"

We ran over to the gym and began playing.

Out of the blue I heard the words: "Ted, what are you doing?"

I turned and saw a student who was obviously taking her faculty pretending job very seriously.

"Who are you?" I asked.

"I'm Ruth and I'm the Registrar. You cannot play basketball when you're supposed to be in industrial arts," she answered.

"Ruth, go do your job and I'll do mine," I said.

She wouldn't leave and insisted we stop playing basketball. I finally couldn't take any more of this do-gooder and I said very calmly, "Ruth, go to hell".

She gasped and rushed out toward the office.

It didn't take long for the real principal to show up. I was scolded and suspended for another week. During that week, I worked with the farm manager.

I had been at Armona for about six weeks and was suspended for two of those. Things were really not going very well for me.

I had lived for the last four weeks at Kenny's house, and one night my parents showed up. They asked if I would like to go back to MBA. I said yes. They had talked to the school and they had agreed to take me back on a probationary status. I think they were embarrassed that I was living with Kenny's family, and sending me back to MBA got me out of everybody's hair.

SECOND CHANCE

I returned to MBA immediately and things actually went quite well. There were only five or six weeks left in the school year and I managed to keep out of trouble for the most part—until the very end.

The junior class was tasked with a variety of activities to honor the seniors. We, the juniors, were at the auditorium practicing on the Thursday afternoon for the weekend graduation activities. Mr. Peters was the coordinator. His son, aged about six or seven, was playing around with a pole, like a pole vaulter, when he wiped out.

Everyone laughed.

Mr. Peters rushed over to me and gave me a royal chewing out about being so disrespectful. I had made a resolution to stay out of trouble, so I remained silent. He finally walked away.

After a few minutes, Mr. Peters lined us up for the grand entry. Meanwhile, I was fuming, and getting madder by the minute.

Then he said loudly: "Ok, let's go."

We started marching in and he suddenly yelled: "Hold it. Where's the organ?"

"It's right over there, can't you see it?" I blurted out.

He lost his temper and threw me out of the line.

That evening was the junior/senior beach party. I wasn't sure if I was supposed to go, based on my altercation with Mr. Peters, but I decided I would arrive late so that the beach activities would have already started.

As I was walking along the narrow road to the beach, a car hit my left leg. I fell to the ground and immediately looked up to see that it was Mr. Peters driving the car. I jumped up and tried to run, but fell back to the ground with a debilitating charley horse. I sat there for a few moments trying to regain my composure.

Before long, a girl in my class ran up and asked if I was okay? I said I was, and got up to try to walk it off.

Seeing Mr. Peters at the party laughing and cutting up infuriated me. I glared at him the whole time, and he did everything to avoid eye contact. I think we both knew it wasn't over.

After the party Mr. Peters was standing at the dividing point, where the girls went left and the boys went right to their respective residence halls. I lagged behind everyone else. I approached Mr. Peters and asked if he knew he had hit me? He said he hadn't hit me. I walked up and slapped him as hard as I could. He stared at me for a second and then walked away. I dearly wished he had thrown a punch.

Two weeks later I received the dreaded letter informing me I would not be welcomed back at MBA.

Summer break had arrived and I was in a dilemma about my future. I wasn't getting along with my parents and I couldn't go back to the school where all my friends were.

However, I was lucky enough to get a summer job at a government rest home and I needed a car. I was told that an elderly lady in our church had one that she wanted to sell. It was a 1938 Dodge sedan. Tim and I went to look at it and she wanted one hundred dollars. We offered her fifty and she agreed. Before we left with the car she told us that this car had been her baby and we shouldn't drive it over twenty-five miles per hour. We told her we would take good care of it.

We drove very slowly as we left, but as soon as we were out of sight we squealed the tires and got our new car up to fifty before it started shaking. After some new tires and a wheel balance, we could easily get it to sixty miles per hour. Tim and I loved our car as we could crowd in up to ten friends.

I also signed up to play baseball in the 16-18 league, but I knew I could be asked to work the 3-11 shift at the rest home and that would cut into our ball games. That is exactly what happened and I played very little that summer.

I had sent letters to several SDA schools and was repeatedly denied. I can't imagine why, with my stellar records at MBA and Armona! I decided that I might need to stay home and go to the local high school, so I signed up for summer school to get started.

One night Tim and I were talking about my plight.

"I don't know what to do. Almost every school I have applied to has denied me," I said.

"Why don't you ask God to help," Tim said.

"Are you kidding," I responded.

"Challenge God and see what happens," he said.

"Challenge how?" I asked.

"Put out Gideon's fleece."

That night I prayed silently: "God, if you want me somewhere else besides the local high school, let me get an acceptance letter."

A few days later I received an acceptance letter from Rio Lindo Academy in Healdsburg, California. I couldn't believe it. I didn't really want to go there but I didn't have many options, except to go to the local high school. That would mean staying at home and fighting with my parents.

Rio Lindo was a brand new school and it had the reputation of being a school for rich kids. My parents were really excited about the Rio Lindo possibility and so we took a trip to check it out.

The school looked nice and the boy's residence hall director, Mr. Botimer, seemed really cool.

I asked about sports and he said he loved sports and wouldn't be there if they didn't have any. I started to feel excited, except I hated the thought that I wouldn't know anybody.

I decided that I would try to convince Tim to come with me.

Although he wanted to, he still had the nightmare of his experience at MBA in his head.

He had become very comfortable at Armona and decided to stay at home.

RIO AND THE GORGEOUS BLONDE

⟡

*W*ith the support of my parents, I decided to go to Rio Lindo. My dad and I had some great talks that summer. He convinced me to try to forget about this past year and all the difficulties I had encountered. Going to a new school could be a great way for starting over. I agreed with him.

As a going away gift he bought me a new baseball glove, the very one I had wanted for a long time. I really loved and idolized my dad. Sometimes I felt sorry for him because I knew he and mom disagreed on so many issues. If she had known about the glove, she would have been quite unhappy.

When school started, I settled into my room and registered for classes in a very timely manner. Everything seemed so organized. Since I had just finished senior history at summer school, I was able to take some electives, like architectural drafting. Mr. Canty, the history teacher, was looking for a student to grade papers and he offered me the job. Of course, I said yes.

I couldn't believe how things were working out. If only Tim could have been there with me.

The first week of school is always an adjustment. I was now a senior and my roommate was a freshman. He followed me around asking the questions a three-year-old would ask his dad.

I didn't know anybody and I was really lonely. There were recreational activities in the evenings but I felt so alone it didn't really matter.

Mr. Botimer offered me a second job buffing the hallway floors. My parents were so glad to get me out of the house that they hadn't pushed me about getting work. I took the job to do my part in helping with the costs. I had worked all of my life, so I really didn't mind.

Then a girl named Linda was hired to help me with the reading and grading of history papers. She had a great sense of humor and we laughed a lot, but more importantly, she knew lots of kids and she helped me to meet others. The loneliness I had felt was becoming a distant memory.

Then my heart skipped a beat! As I was going through the cafeteria line, I saw a beautiful blonde girl who was serving meals. I said hello but she didn't respond, just continued doing her job. The next day I asked Linda if she knew the blonde girl who was serving on the boy's side.

She laughed and said: "I sure do, she's my roommate."

"She's a doll," I said.

"Yea, well, she has a boyfriend," Linda responded.

Her name is Suzy, and Linda told her that I had asked about her.

A few days later, when Linda and I were grading papers, Suzy walked in.

WOW! She was even more beautiful without her cafeteria apron and hair net. The three of us sat around goofing off. I was relieved that Suzy was not as stuck up as she appeared to be in the café. It was an enjoyable day.

Even though I had made a few friends, for the first six weeks at Rio I was really homesick and began calling my parents to see if I could come home. The answer was always no. I decided that I had to convince Tim to join me. Finally, he agreed to come after the first six-week grading period.

When he arrived, everything immediately turned around. I was much happier, and Tim seemed to fit right in. As it turned out, I gained two new roommates. As well as Tim, Gary had also just enrolled at Rio and joined us. Gary was a rather mischievous character and we all hit it off immediately. We didn't get much school work done, but the three of us were having a lot of fun.

Sports at Rio were all intramurals, not interscholastic. They were however very organized. Tim and I volunteered to be co-captains in the flag football segment so that we were able to play together. We, of course, also chose Gary.

Our team was very good and we went undefeated, as did another team that included three seniors who had been at Rio for several years: Roger, Cliff, and Bill. They didn't like Tim and me, mostly because we were the new guys and an obvious challenge to them on the field. We were scheduled to play their team in the last game.

As expected, it was a very close game. We were behind by five points, but were driving for a touchdown with time running out. I was playing quarterback and Tim was one of my receivers. It was fourth down, and our ball on their five-yard line. Tim ran a perfect route and I threw the ball to him just as I had a thousand times before. The throw was a little high and Tim went up and made the catch. The official raised his hands and the victory was ours.

But wait....

Tim was talking to the official—who then began waving his hands to indicate the catch was no good. Tim was the most honest person I have ever known, and he had admitted that he had come down on the line.

Gary and I wanted to kill him.

Then, the most amazing thing happened. Roger, Cliff, and Bill came over and thanked us for being honest. From that point forward, they became our friends.

A few days later at the boy's club activity night, we played a game called bombardment; a dodgeball game that is played with many balls. The game requires everyone to be honest about being hit and therefore taking themselves out of the game. The seniors and freshmen played the juniors and sophomores.

In the first game, one junior kept being hit but wouldn't withdraw from the game. He was a big kid with a big mouth; his name was Ed. Roger said he wasn't someone to mess with.

In the second game, Ed did the same thing and we lost yet again.

I don't like to lose, especially when someone is cheating. I walked over to Ed and reminded him that when you are hit, you get off the floor.

"I'll get off the floor when I feel like it and what are you going to do about it?" he replied haughtily.

The gym fell silent as everybody watched to see what I would do.

I slapped him hard. He just stood there staring in disbelief.

I was ready to do battle. Our eyes locked on to each other. I could see he wanted to fight, but also appeared afraid. He'd probably never been challenged like this before.

He decided against a fight and slowly walked away. He played fair after that and we creamed them.

Mr. Botimer called me in after the game and told me I was out of line when I hit Ed.

I was not going to let this situation derail my senior year. Things were going too good and it was up to me to make sure it stayed that way. I agreed that I was out of line and I apologized. I asked if he wanted me to apologize to Ed.

"I'll leave that up to you. The truth of the matter is that Ed will probably be a better person for the experience."

I never apologized to Ed.

First semester went surprisingly well. My grades were up, the sports were great, and I had two friends, Tim and Gary, to share the ups and downs of life. We had a lot of fun and although we did get into a little mischief, it was nothing to be suspended for.

One day we caught a lizard and let it go at chapel, right before the main prayer when everyone was on their knees. As expected, an earth-shattering scream rang out. The lizard had crawled on one of the girls.

Another time we caught some H-bees (drones that don't sting) and tied thread around their necks. We let them go at chapel and they flew around slowly, creating quite a show.

Thankfully, we were not busted for either escapade.

A few weeks later, I was in study hall in the library. Ms. Morrel was an old, old, typical librarian. She demanded total order and silence. I went to get a drink, and on my way back got down on the floor and began looking for my contact lens. Before long there were several students helping me. The only catch; I didn't wear contact lenses.

I finally pretended to find it and put on a short theatrical show to put it back in my eye.

I didn't get suspended for this, but instead wasn't allowed to go on the senior trip. I thought this was a little harsh but accepted it as my own doing.

During second semester, Tim began dating Linda, the girl I worked with in the history department. I really liked Linda and thought they were a good match. One day Linda asked if I would like to go with Suzy, her, and Tim to the Saturday night function.

I knew that Suzy had a boyfriend but he was no longer in school. I really wanted to date her, but knew I would just be going as her friend. I told Linda that I would go.

We had a great time and a lot of laughs. Suzy wasn't only a doll, but also a lot of fun. I wished she was available, but for now, just being friends would have to do.

A month or so later, Linda asked if I could do Suzy a favor. A guy she wasn't crazy about had asked her to the senior/junior picnic and she told him she already had a date. Linda asked if I would like to be her date.

WOW! Would I!

We spent the day together and Suzy was absolutely great. She was fun, easy to talk to, and just comfortable from the start. I found out she was now single, having broken up with her boyfriend. I knew right then and there that I was not going to let this girl get away.

Until the end of the school year, we saw each other as much as possible.

One evening I walked her back to her dorm and as I said goodbye, I snuck up close and gave her a quick kiss. She gave me a small smile, then turned and walked up the steps to her dorm.

I was smitten by this girl.

As I was graduating and Suzy was a junior, it appeared this was a relationship that was not going to be easy going forward. She was so special, and I didn't want to lose her.

That summer Tim and I drove the five hours from Dinuba to Ukiah on several occasions to see Linda and Suzy.

I also returned to my job at the government rest home.

I was planning on going to a university in Southern California and rooming with Roger, but then, another setback; I got a letter from the university denying my acceptance.

I wasn't sure what I was going to do. If it weren't for the Vietnam War and losing my student deferment, I might have just stayed out a year and waited for Suzy.

ANDREWS UNIVERSITY

*C*lyde had graduated from college and was headed to a ministerial program at Andrews University in Berrien Springs, Michigan. My parents decided that's where they wanted me to go. I really hated to move that far away from Suzy, however as they had agreed to pay for it and I thought it would be fun to hang around with Clyde, I agreed to go.

Clyde had been away from home for most of the past seven years. He was four years ahead of me in school and had taken summer jobs that kept him away from home. In short, I really didn't know Clyde all that well. When he had come home at Christmas and other special occasions, Tim and I had spent most of the time teasing him. He was always a good sport about it.

When Clyde and I arrived at Andrews, it felt like I was in a foreign country; everything was strange.

The men's residence hall was a great looking building called Meyer Hall. When I went to register for my room, the attendant at the desk told me that I wasn't in Meyer Hall, but in Burman Hall.

That was okay, but where was Burman?

With directions in hand, I walked through the darkness to an old,

old building. It looked like something from a horror movie; one of those old buildings that would probably fall down if you sneezed.

I was allocated a room, and a roommate.

The next day I went through the miserable experience of registering for classes. This began at the gym.

I had waited in line for about two hours before I finally reached the starting table and they asked for my financial papers. What financial papers?

I was given the instructions I needed to get them from the administration building. I stood in line for another couple of hours and when I was finally able to talk to someone, yes, you guessed it, I was in the wrong line and needed to go to the finance office to arrange for payment. Then return to the administration building with my financial agreement.

By the time I had my clearance to register for classes, registration had closed for the day.

I was finally able to register for classes the next day.

As I wasn't sure of what I wanted to major in, some well-meaning class advisor placed me in chemistry, world civilization, French, and English.

I went to my first class at 9:00 a.m. the next day—I was the only one there. It turns out that the class only meets each Monday, Wednesday, and Friday—and not on Tuesdays.

Surely things could only get better!

That evening there was a tryout for the freshman football intramural team.

Okay, now we're talking!

After the tryouts, the captain told us the team would be posted at 3:00 p.m. the next day in Meyer Hall. I hustled over to Meyer Hall and looked at the chosen team.

My name was NOT on it!

In all of my short life, I have never tried out for a team and not made it. I was quite shaken and I really despised this whole experience so far. So much for things getting better.

Not making the freshman football team was disappointing, however it might have been a blessing in disguise.

I decided to take a walk around Meyer Hall. While wandering around in the basement, I came across a large room full of weights and other equipment, even mirrors on the walls.

The room was empty except for one rather large guy wearing a tank top, head band, and wild sweat pants. He stopped and stared at me.

"What do you want?" he asked abruptly.

"Just looking around," I said as I slowly backed out of the room.

The weight room was not officially open until later that night. I learned that the guy's name was Albert and he worked there.

I had never lifted weights and was intrigued, especially as I had not made the freshman football team. That night I went down to the weight room and it was buzzing.

Then I saw Albert. Actually, I heard him before I saw him. He was walking around in small circles growling and making a scene as he contemplated what looked to be an enormous amount of weight on a bar.

He bent down, grabbed the bar, took three or four loud breaths, and then attempted to pull the bar straight up to his waist (dead lift). When the bar was about half way up, he trembled briefly and then screamed louder than I had ever heard anyone scream, and dropped the weights. He walked around the room huffing and puffing and I thought the theatrics would never end.

Finally, he sat down and stared at the bar from across the room.

Then a smaller guy walked over to the same bar, grabbed it, and without making a sound, lifted it all the way up to his waist. He held it for a couple of seconds and then lowered it slowly to the ground, all the time remaining in complete control. I was amazed.

I walked over and introduced myself; his name was Tom Smith. He was about my height, but well built. I had always wanted to work out with weights but didn't know how. I asked if he could help me with a weightlifting program and he seemed excited about the prospect of being my tutor. He taught me how to lift correctly and how to breathe. He also put together a weekly workout program and introduced me to a completely new world of nutrition.

Clyde and I spent a lot of time together that first week. He knew how disappointed I was about not making the football team and made a point of being there for me.

It was fun getting to know Clyde. We talked about a lot of things, including my spiritual life. I expressed many concerns about God and the SDA church. Clyde was a great listener and seemed genuinely concerned about me. It felt really good to have him there with me, especially as I didn't know a sole and it looked like sports wasn't going to be in my immediate future.

Clyde had his own reservations about this place, and worried how well he would do in the theology program. Clyde had always been a good student and I expected he would do great.

Each week Clyde and I went to church together at Pioneer Memorial, the university church.

On the third Saturday, I decided to play a trick on Clyde. We were sitting in our pew with Clyde next to the aisle on his right. I took out a small piece of paper and wrote the following:

I pressed a kiss up to her lips
I could not help but linger
And as my hand ran thru her hair
A cootie bit my finger

Clyde was keeping a close eye on me the whole time I was writing. When I was finished, I showed him the poem. When he had finished reading it, he gave a little wry smile and said, "cute".

I then took the poem and wrote at the bottom, by Clyde Evans. There was no longer a smile on his face. He tried to grab it but I was ready for him and jerked it away.

I folded the paper and put it into a tithe envelope. I wrote on the envelope: For the pastor. Personal. I put the envelope in my coat lapel pocket.

Clyde of course had seen what I had written on the envelope, and I could see the wheels turning as he contemplated what his crazy younger brother was going to do. I knew he was hoping that when the ushers were passing the offering plates, the one in our row would come to him last so that he could retrieve the tithe envelope.

It seemed like forever before they finally took the offering. As the plate got to our row, Clyde seemed to gain some relief as it was indeed coming down the row toward him. When it got to me I noticed that the usher was still a couple of rows ahead, so I just held on to the plate until he was right beside Clyde.

The usher, an elderly gentleman, looked down at me and I reached into my pocket and took out the envelope, slowly placing it onto the plate, face down, and passed it to Clyde. Clyde's hand went up as if he was going to grab the envelope, then his hand stopped and began to tremble. The usher reached down and took the offering plate with the tithe envelope still in place.

Once outside the church I could see that Clyde was truly angry, even though he was trying to suppress it. He was so mad that he looked at me and called me the worst name he had ever called me.

"You're incorrigible," he fumed.

"Thank you," I said. I wasn't insulted because I had no idea what incorrigible meant.

Clyde was such a good and caring person, and it was proven once again when he let me off so lightly for what I had done.

The next week Clyde and I met for church again. We sat in almost the same place as the week before. As the offering was taken, I'm sure Clyde was having some thoughts about the adventure of last week.

The plate came from the same direction and I immediately passed the plate to Clyde. After he gave it to the usher, I reached into my lapel pocket and pulled out a tithe envelope. I gave it to Clyde face down. He flipped it over and there was the envelope that said: For the pastor. Personal. He quickly opened it to find the silly poem.

While he still wasn't happy with me, he confessed years later that he had told that story many times, and even used it in a sermon.

DROP OUT AND TROUBLE

*S*chool began badly and it went downhill from there.

I dropped out after ten weeks and went back to California. The best thing about those ten weeks, other than getting reacquainted with Clyde, was the friendship I had with Tom Smith and the weightlifting program he had tutored me through. I began the program weighing 165 pounds and ten weeks later, I weighed 188. I felt great. I was bigger, stronger, and faster.

Maybe not making the football team was a blessing.

My first stop was to see Suzy. The first thing she said to me was: "Wow! You've got muscles."

She was as beautiful as ever. I knew I couldn't stay for long. The academy had such strict rules that I could barely even visit with her. I was in love with her and hated the thought that I might lose her.

When I got back home, it was NOT a joyous occasion. My parents were very disappointed that I had dropped out of college. To make matters worse, Tim had also dropped out. This had to be embarrassing for parents who were both teachers.

The first thing I did was apply for my old job at the government rest home, called Sequoia Home. They were short-staffed and Tim and I were hired immediately.

Secondly, I bought a car. It was an older Austin Healey convertible. I loved that car and couldn't wait to show it to Suzy.

I told Tim all about Andrews University and about Notre Dame University in South Bend, Indiana, which is only about twenty-five miles from Andrews. In that area, everything sports was about Notre Dame. That particular year the Fighting Irish football team was really good and ranked number one in the country.

As the season wound down, Notre Dame and Michigan State were both undefeated and scheduled to play in about two weeks.

I couldn't wait to watch the game, but of course it was on a Saturday, the sacred worship day for SDAs.

On the day of the big game, Tim and I left church and snuck home to watch it. It had only been on for a few minutes when dad walked in. He was surprisingly calm—he walked over to the TV, turned it off, and then sat down.

"Boys," he said, "here's how this works. We want you to live with us, and if you decide you want to live with us, you must follow our rules. We are all SDAs and you must respect that if you decide to stay. Church is a requirement and Saturday will be respected as the Lord's Day. We do not watch TV on the Lord's Day."

I didn't have the courage to tell him that as far as I was concerned I wasn't an SDA.

I couldn't believe how bad I felt. I loved my dad and never wanted to disrespect him. I apologized and so did Tim.

A week later, right after church, Tim and I asked dad if we could go over to Sequoia Home and see some of our old buddies. He said it was okay, but not to take too long to get home for lunch. We both had our favorite residents; mine was a man named Elmer. Elmer loved Coke and I often bought him one as a treat while I sat and listened to his war stories.

When Elmer had finished his Coke, I said goodbye. Tim and I then headed for home.

In our home, the meal after church was always special, but today when we walked in the house, the table wasn't set and there didn't appear to be a special meal in the making.

Dad was sitting on the couch reading and mom was playing the organ. Mom was obviously out of sorts because she was wearing, "the look".

Unfortunately, from the time I was eight or nine, I often made things worse by saying or doing little things that didn't help the situation when she was in one of her moods. Today would be no different. She had a strong will and a fierce temper, and so did I.

"Where's lunch?" I asked.

"If you want lunch fix it yourself," she said. "There's stuff in the fridge."

"Oh boy, this will be fun," I said loudly to Tim, knowing it would really get my mother's goat.

I opened the fridge and said: "Hey, do you like pickles, Tim? And how about cheese."

Mom came around the fridge door and grabbed the block of cheese, but I held on and jerked it out of her hand. She stumbled back against dad.

"Get him, Ed," she screamed.

Dad and I stared at each other for a moment.

Mom screamed at him again, "GET HIM, ED"!

He put up his fists and began swinging. I was too big and too strong, and quickly had him pinned up against the wall, pummeling him with punches.

The next thing I knew, Tim was on my back screaming for me to quit. Mom and dad hustled back to their bedroom where they called the police.

When the police arrived, they began badgering me and calling me names.

"So, you think you're a big man and can beat up your parents," one said.

He was really trying to get me to take a swing at him. I sat there and took it. They told me not to move and went back to talk to mom and dad. When they returned they asked me to stand and turn around. I was handcuffed and taken to the police station.

Sitting in a cell that afternoon, all kinds of emotions were running through my head. I was embarrassed, exasperated, and angry all at the same time.

I hated that I had this physical altercation with my dad. I had always loved and admired him. I knew it wasn't his fault, but he had no choice. I also knew that I had provoked the fight. I sat there that afternoon and evening thinking: Why is my life such a mess.

This was one of the lowest points of my life. I had gone from totally defiant to totally defeated.

I sat in my cell for the next seven or eight hours contemplating my life and how miserable much of it had been. I wondered why I should keep on living. I considered suicide; mom would have to live with that for the rest of her life. I thought this could be the ultimate punishment for her.

If it were not for my love for Suzy and Tim....

That night the police opened up my cell and took me home. They told me not to talk to my folks, but just get my stuff and leave. I was not to return home without permission.

I did as I was instructed.

ON MY OWN

I tried to sleep in my car, but it was a two-seater and not very comfortable. I had three other options, but none were perfect.

The first was to stay with my friends, Mike and Duane, who lived on a farm. In one corner of an old barn was the boxing ring that we had used for practice when I was boxing. It was still there. With my sleeping bag and the heavy mats in the ring, it was fairly comfortable. But the barn had no heat and, being November, the nights could get pretty cold. There was also no electricity to be able to have a space heater and no rest room or shower. Mike and Duane would sometimes sneak me into their house when their parents were out, but I had to be careful as their mom was best friends with my mom.

Then there was the Junior Academy Gym, it had mats, heat, and a bathroom. Although it was locked, I knew how to get in. I also knew that if I was caught the police would be called and it could be a real mess. So, I rarely stayed there unless it was going to be really cold.

I would also stay at Sequoia Home. The home was housed in two buildings, and there were two additional buildings that were empty. I would sneak into one of the empty buildings to sleep, although I didn't like to stay there as I knew it could jeopardize my job.

As time went on, I tried to save as much money as I could so that I could visit Suzy. I went to her place for a few days at Christmas, staying until I had to go back to work.

How great those few days were. I had a bed, heat, shower, and really good food; not to mention my time with Suzy. I had lost about 10 to 15 pounds by then.

After my time with Suzy, things went from bad to worse.

The principal at the academy caught me sleeping in the gym. He was stern and laid down the law; I was not to stay there again or they would press charges for breaking and entering.

A few days later, I was caught sleeping in one of the vacant buildings at the rest home. They wrote me up and told me that if it happened again I would lose my job.

This was the beginning of January and it was cold. The barn was my only remaining choice. On very cold nights, I parked my car inside and slept in it with the engine running and the heater on.

Tim had started a new job working at the city recreation department. They had a big room with pool tables, ping-pong, etc. I would go there almost every day and hang out with Tim. Usually I could take a much-needed nap on a couch until I had to go to work, and even take a sponge bath in the rest room.

One day as I left the recreation department, a car drove by and a guy flipped me off. I didn't recognize the car so I ignored it and kept going. The car made a quick U-turn and drove up behind me. I pulled over into a vacant lot and watched in my rearview mirror as he got out of his car and hustled up to mine. As I opened my door, I saw that his fists were knuckled up.

I jumped out and slugged him in the mouth. It split his lip and knocked him to the ground. He crawled over and wrapped his arms around my legs. It was on! I went for him with all I had. Suddenly I heard a wild scream and a woman was running toward me with a cement block held over her head. She threw it at me. I ducked, got up and jumped into my car, and took off.

I had no idea who this was, or what it was all about, but I thought his girlfriend would probably have put up a better fight than he did.

I told Tim about what had happened.

"Oh yea, I know him. I had to kick him out of the recreation center. He probably thought it was me in the car."

A day or so later Tim told me that he had been walking along the sidewalk in town when this same guy came toward him. The guy looked pretty beat up and when he saw Tim, he crossed over to the other side of the street.

"He thinks I beat him up," Tim said.

Mike, Duane, Tim and I all played in the City League Basketball league from mid-January through to March. I changed my work hours to dayshifts. While I was super excited about playing, it also provided a great opportunity to have a regular shower.

A tournament was held at the end of the season. Our team had finished second in regular league play and now had a chance to win it all. We won our first two games and were now set to play against the number one team for the league championship.

The first game had been very close and we expected this one to be the same; and it was. We were behind by one point with time running out. Mike brought the ball down and fed it to our big man who made a move to shoot, but instead passed it out to Tim. Tim was our best outside shooter. He got the ball and took the shot. I thought it would never come down. Swish, nothing but net.

We had won!

After the game, my parents walked up to me.

"Hi Ted, how are you doing?" Mom asked.

I had not seen them for almost five months. I had lost about 25 pounds since I had left home and I looked terrible. My mom started crying and said that they wanted me to come home.

I tried to act nonchalant about the offer but, the truth be known, I was thrilled to hear those words. I agreed to give it a try.

During my first meal at home, I remember thinking that I didn't remember mom's cooking to be so good.

Things actually went pretty well this time around.

THE TRIP FROM HELL

⚜

a month or so after I had moved back home, my parents asked if I would be willing to go on a trip with my friend David and his parents, Nick and Edith. They were having a difficult time with David and were hoping that I could help.

They were going to Ohio to pick up some buses at a manufacturing plant. If I would go, they would be able to pick up an additional bus; and I would be paid. The trip was going to take eight or nine days. David was a lifelong friend so I arranged to take leave from the rest home and agreed to go. They were to pick me up first thing Wednesday morning.

Wednesday morning came and they didn't come. I tried to call them but there was no answer. Later that day they called to say they had had some problems and they would be going the next morning and would pick me up at 10:00 a.m.

Thursday 10:00 a.m. came and went. I had missed two days of work and was ready to bail on this whole deal.

I told my dad how frustrated I was and he asked me to be patient as he was sure there was a good reason. That afternoon they showed up and we set off.

Instead of going to Sacramento and then east on Interstate 80, we went west to the Napa Valley and to Pacific Union College (PUC) where David's brother and sister were students.

I kept asking myself; what have I got myself into?

We agreed to meet in front of the dorm first thing the next morning to continue our trip. Yea right, I thought. I found a friend in the dorm and slept on his floor.

The next morning I waited in the lobby and nobody showed up. Late in the morning, I started walking around campus to try to find them.

Behind the women's dorm, I saw their car. I looked around and saw Nick screaming at David. Suddenly Nick began hitting him. David cowered and didn't fight back. I wasn't sure what to do so I ran over screaming at Nick to stop. He did, but he had this horrific look on his face.

Oh, Lord, I thought, what have I got myself into?

I desperately wanted to get out of this mess. I called my dad and told him I couldn't do this. He told me they really needed me and encouraged me to stay with it.

We left that afternoon and drove all night to Salt Lake City, Utah.

It was Saturday morning and Nick was looking for a SDA church. We found it and we all went in; low and behold, it was a black SDA church. Nick turned right back around and we all followed. He was looking for a particular church and this wasn't it.

He found a pay phone and located the church he was looking for. The minister was an acquaintance who had been a pastor at our church in California a couple of years earlier.

After church, some local members invited us to their home for lunch, but David's parents were waiting on an invitation from our former pastor.

Eventually the pastor did invite us over. He and his wife were good people and good Christians. At our church in California, everybody loved them. He also worked with my dad in the Pathfinders Club.

After lunch, having learned we had driven all night, they invited us to take a nap in their home. We took them up on their offer and slept until suppertime. After staying for supper, we continued on our trip. I was so embarrassed.

We drove for the next two days without a break and arrived at Andrews University in Berrien Springs, Michigan, on Monday night. Their oldest daughter lived there and that's where we stayed.

Tuesday morning David and I dressed up like hippies and went to find my brother Clyde, who was in the ministerial program at Andrews. We sat down in the hallway outside his class and waited. When Clyde's class ended, he walked down the hall with two of his classmates, right past David and me.

As he walked by, I said in my deepest voice, but not real loud "Clyde". They kept walking. About twenty feet down the hall Clyde suddenly stopped and walked back to us. He stared for a moment, trying to register what he was seeing.

"What *are* you two doing?" he asked.

Then we all broke into laughter.

Later, after David returned to his parents, I filled Clyde in on the whole situation.

As it turned out, Nick decided we weren't in that big of a hurry and we spent the whole week there, which was really bad for me.

I called my supervisor at work; she said to keep her informed on how things were going and she would get by.

I stayed with Clyde the whole week and we had fun exploring and just catching up.

On the following Monday, after a six-day break, we headed for Lima, Ohio, to finally pick up the buses.

David's parents and I each drove a bus, with David coming with me. Nick gave me strict instructions about how I should drive, and to follow his every move, like lane changes, etc. He towed their car behind his bus.

We drove for a few hours and then left the freeway, shortly arriving at a small town to stay with David's relatives.

How could this keep happening? We were never going to get back home at this rate; I was going to lose my job. I had now been off work for thirteen days.

That night I talked to Edith about how unfair they were being to me. She was a sweet lady and expressed her remorse, but told me Nick was in charge and there was nothing she could do. I knew she was right and I felt sorry for her.

The next day we began our journey midmorning and made good time. Close to St. Louis, I thought; okay, now we're making up some time. I thought Edith must have had a talk with Nick.

Early that afternoon we stopped for fuel. Next to the gas station was a flea market. Nick told us that they were going to take a break and walk around the flea market. He said we could come with them or stay on the bus.

Are you kidding! I was livid.

David and I had a quick discussion about our options.

"David, I've had enough! I want to take our bus and head for home." I said.

"I'm with you, let's go!" he replied.

I started the bus and we headed out. I knew Nick was going to be out of his mind when he found out, but I didn't care.

We were in Missouri, heading west with a full tank of gas, and it felt good.

We drove until late that night and then pulled over so I could sleep. I didn't sleep long before we were on the road again.

We were now in Oklahoma and making good time.

Suddenly, David said he saw buses behind us and they were catching up fast. I could see them in my mirrors now and then as we drove over the rolling terrain.

I was driving as fast as the bus would allow, but I soon realized I couldn't outrun them. On the other side of a small rise was an off-ramp.

Hidden by the shallow valley, I took the off-ramp and ran the stop sign, making a sharp right-hand turn. A bit too sharp! The bus rose up on two wheels. I swerved and managed to save it, slammed on the brakes, and skidded to a stop.

I could not believe I almost flipped the bus.

We continued along a small road and hid the bus behind some

trees. I jumped out to check the freeway. When the buses went by, there were four of them. It wasn't David's parents.

We jumped back into our bus and headed out. Wow! The adrenaline was pumping. I still couldn't believe I almost wrecked the bus, and it wasn't even them.

That evening we had made it into New Mexico. I didn't know the area and we were getting low on fuel. I had some of my own money, so filled up at a gas station and bought some food. It took everything I had and I was now broke. We sat there and ate hungrily as we had eaten very little since leaving David's parents behind.

"We're busted!" David blurted out.

A Highway Patrol car pulled up behind us with its lights flashing. A patrol officer came onto the bus and asked if I was Ted Evans.

"You have been accused of stealing this bus," he said. "Your friend's parents are a couple of hours behind you. You are not allowed to move this bus. If you do, we will arrest you. As of now, I will let you work this out with his parents, but again," he reiterated, "do not move this bus!"

After the patrol officer left, I couldn't believe I had just used all of my money to fill this bus. David and I discussed our options.

"My dad is going to beat the hell out of me," David kept saying.

"David, that is not going to happen," I said.

I was trying my best to act brave, but I knew we could be in for a wild experience. Nick wasn't a big man, but he was physically in shape as his normal job was felling and cutting trees.

I had already seen him beat up David and knew he would do it again if he had the chance, and possibly me, too. I began to contemplate what I would do if he did attack me.

"We don't have to let him on the bus. We'll lock the back door and he can't open the front with me holding the door handle," I said. "If your dad does get on the bus, you stay in the back and don't say anything. I will take responsibility for everything."

David agreed.

A short time later, Nick jumped out of his bus and ran over to ours. I held the door handle as he was pulling for all he was worth, all the time screaming wildly at me. Finally, he stopped and ran to the back door. A scary thought then crossed my mind. Is it possible he has a duplicate key to our bus? As it turned out, he didn't.

He walked around the bus a few times threatening me and David, and then he went back to his bus to talk to Edith.

Soon Edith came over and asked if she could come in and talk with us. I opened the door, while carefully watching for Nick. Edith was very emotional, but also very sweet. She told us about their plan.

"We are going north, about a three-hour drive, drop off the two buses, and then drive back in the car. You can come with us or stay here until we get back to collect this bus."

"We'll discuss it and let you know." I said.

"Nick also wants to talk to you. He is cooling off and won't do anything crazy." Edith added.

"I saw Nick beat up David and I'm not going to allow that to happen again," I said.

"Let's just give him a little time and he will be fine," she assured me.

A short time later, Edith said Nick was ready to talk.

"David, stay in the back of the bus, do not move or speak," I said.

He agreed and I told Edith that Nick could come on the bus. I opened the front door and then moved back in front of David.

Nick calmly walked across to our bus. He climbed aboard and began walking toward me.

"David," he yelled. "Come here."

I motioned for David to stay put.

"David is not going anywhere with you. He's staying with me." I replied.

"Get out of my way," he yelled.

He came closer, wearing that same wild horrific look I had seen after he'd beaten David at PUC.

"Get out of my way," he screamed, his hands knuckled up into fists.

"Nick, I'm not like David, I *will* fight," I said. "If you want him, you will have to go through me."

"Get out of my way," he screamed again.

I was praying; please God, let this end—peacefully.

I tried to appear unafraid, but in truth, I was petrified. If we did get into a fight, it would be a real embarrassment for everyone at home.

He looked possessed and kept screaming at me, getting closer and closer. I put my fists up and kept on praying; God, help me.

I stared at him and stood my ground. He was now standing a foot away.

"*Get out of my way*," he screamed.

I didn't move.

After what seemed like an eternity, Nick slowly turned and walked off the bus.

Unbelievable, I thought. Thank you, Lord!

Edith then came and asked us what we were going to do.

"We will not go with you, and if we're not here when you get back, we have moved on." I said.

As soon as they left, we picked up our stuff and began hitchhiking.

We got lucky and were picked up by a caravan of four or five buses. We were able to ride with them as far as Barstow, California.

When we left them, we walked to the Greyhound bus station. One problem—we had no money.

I asked a man if I could borrow a dime to use the pay phone and made a collect call to home. My mom answered. She agreed to wire the money for the bus tickets to get us home. When I hung up, four quarters dropped out of the telephone.

"There is a God," I said to David.

We went to a little dinner nearby and ordered two grilled cheese sandwiches and two small cartons of milk. It came to ninety-eight cents. After we had eaten, David and I felt amazingly full.

JUST GIVE ME A CHANCE

That summer I was invited to play on an elite baseball team representing our town. I could not have been more excited at the opportunity.

A number of the players were being looked at by major league teams. They had much more experience than I did, having played varsity high school and college baseball, while I went to SDA schools with no interscholastic sports.

As the summer progressed, I became more comfortable with the higher caliber of play. One of the main games would be against the preeminent powerhouse team in the region—Selma. They had always had exceptionally good players, and two of their pitchers had been courted by several professional baseball franchises. We all knew that there would be a number of scouts at the game, which made it even more exciting.

We practiced hard, and as the game drew closer, we were convinced that we could beat them. The big game couldn't come soon enough.

The day finally arrived and Selma scored four runs in the first inning. While this was a blow to us, we really felt good about our team. We had prepared for a battle and our confidence and determination were still intact.

Our dogged practice and our determination paid off—the final score was Dinuba 14 to Selma 4.

During the game, I hit two home runs and a triple. The local paper published a great article on our victory, and highlighted my performance.

After the game, several scouts came over and talked to me and my dad. The questions they asked were along the lines of: Who are you? Why don't we know you? Which high school did you attend?

That last question was embarrassing for a kid who had attended five high schools.

One of the scouts asked he if could visit our home and talk about my future.

My dad made it very clear to each scout that we were SDAs and he and my mom would not sign for me to play professional baseball based on religious convictions.

One scout asked if he could send some information and possibly a proposal. He wanted to get some references from the coaches before he made an offer.

"You can send it, but you might as well know our position is nonnegotiable," said Dad.

A couple of weeks later I received a letter and a proposal. That night I talked to my parents about it. They were silent as I laid out my rationale for wanting to play professional baseball.

The main points I made: I'm nineteen years old and should be allowed to make my own decisions; This has been my dream since I was a little boy; The Lord has given me this talent, I should be allowed to use it; and, If it's the wrong thing to do, let me decide that after I have tried it.

"Let us think about it," was the answer I received.

Later, dad talked to me about the situation privately. He expressed how proud he was that I had received an offer from a major league team. He asked me to pray about it, and consider all of the ramifications. He and mom would do the same.

I spent a number of long days wondering if my dreams might actually come true.

Finally, it was time to get my answer.

Before the meeting with my parents, I prayed both by myself and with Tim.

My prayer to God was that he would help my parents to see the benefits this opportunity would bring for me, and they would agree to sign.

After I prayed with Tim, he asked, "What if God doesn't think this is the best thing for you?"

That is a possibility I did not want to contemplate.

Mom was in charge of the meeting. She talked about their rationale and the positives and negatives of any decision they made.

At the end of her presentation, she said they could not, with a clear conscience, sign for me.

I was actually not surprised. I thought mom had made a thoughtful and courteous presentation and I felt somewhat respectful of their decision.

But I was not happy.

PACIFIC UNION COLLEGE AND
NO MONEY

*E*arlier that summer I had turned in my application to attend Pacific Union College (PUC) in the Napa Valley.

I had always loved the Bible story of Gideon and how he had challenged the Lord by putting out his fleece.

So, I challenged the Lord: "If you want me to go to PUC, a Christian school, let me be accepted."

Of course, the Lord also knew I was desperate to attend PUC because my girlfriend Suzy was going to be there. I felt like I might lose her if she went there without me.

As the summer progressed, I checked the mail each and every day hoping I would hear from PUC.

Tim and I had also applied to the local Junior College (JC).

With the Vietnam War in full swing, we had to go to school to keep our student deferments. Tim was planning to try out for the JC basketball program, and I was planning to do the same with baseball.

The JC started two weeks earlier than PUC, and as I had not heard from PUC, I went ahead and enrolled at the JC.

On Saturday, after two full weeks at the JC, a letter finally arrived from PUC.

No way, I thought. Could this be it? After my baseball dreams were crushed, could this be the door the Lord would open for me?

I had challenged the Lord and I was afraid to open the envelope. Would I once again be denied? And have my dreams of being with Suzy, the girl that I loved, shattered?

I took a deep breath and opened the envelope.

I was accepted to PUC!

Unbelievable! Now what?

Registration was Sunday, tomorrow! I had no money. My last check from Sequoia Home went to enrolling and buying books at the JC.

I could beg my parents, but they had already made it perfectly clear that I was on my own for schooling because I had dropped out of Andrews the year before.

My car was in the shop with transmission problems, so I had no way of travelling the three hundred miles to PUC.

But wait....

Ronnie, a local SDA friend, was going to PUC. Maybe I could catch a ride with him.

I called Ronnie and he said I could ride with him. He was leaving early Sunday morning.

I talked to my dad and asked him to sell my car when it got out of the shop. I would give this money to PUC as soon as I got it. I figured I could clear at least five hundred dollars when it was sold. He said he would do that for me.

When I walked into the business office at PUC on Sunday morning, I had twenty dollars in my pocket.

The financial advisor laughed when I told her.

"Really, what financial arrangements have you made?" she asked.

"I really only have twenty dollars. What can I do, and who can I talk to?" I asked.

She told me to wait over to the side and she would get back to me.

Soon a man in a suit approached me and invited me into his office. His name was Mr. Manley.

I gave him a brief history, leaving out a few of the gory details, and told him I had enrolled at the local JC as I had not heard from PUC until yesterday.

"Are you willing to work?" he asked.

"Absolutely!" I replied.

"What kind of work have you done?" he asked.

I reeled off a list of jobs I had done and closed with service station attendant.

"Whoa right there," he said. "Can you fix a flat and change the oil in a common car?"

"You bet I can," I said, full of excitement.

"Our service station manager is looking for a student with some experience. Would your parents be willing to sign student loan papers for you?" he asked.

"No. They are upset that I went to Andrews last year and then dropped out. They have told me they would no longer help me in any way." Boy this is going to be tough, I thought.

I then added: "But I have a car that is getting repaired and my dad is going to sell it on my behalf. I am sure I will get at least five hundred dollars for it to go towards enrollment."

"Okay, here's what we are going to do. I'm going to send your parents the papers on the chance that they might change their minds and co-sign for a student loan. If you are willing to put in twenty hours a week at the service station, and you get me the five hundred dollars when the car sells, I am going to allow you to start school," he said.

Wow, I said to myself. This is the most Christian man I have ever known.

He arranged for me to be registered and to buy books.

When I checked in at the dorm they said I would be in the basement. This was the overflow area that had about twenty-five or thirty bunks set up like an army barracks. The other students who were assigned to the basement were really unhappy; some even packed up and left. It wasn't wonderful and there was virtually no security, but I had so little that I wasn't worried about that. I was just thrilled to be here.

That afternoon I saw Suzy and her mom walking toward the girl's dorm. I had been waiting for them and I was thrilled to see Suzy. Her mom seemed a little standoffish. We talked for a few minutes and then Suzy had her registration appointment.

About two days later Duane, my friend from Armona, saw me in the cafeteria.

"Would you like to room with me?" he asked.

"Are you kidding, of course," was my jubilant reply.

Duane had polio when he was a kid and had one weak leg as a result, although he was still a good athlete. He would kid around about it, but privately I knew it really bothered him. We became the best of friends and I was forever grateful he had bailed me out of the basement.

Things went pretty well after that. Suzy and I had some classes together and we enjoyed being free to walk around and talk. College was so liberal compared to SDA high schools.

Work was going well and intramurals were exhilarating. Football was the first intramural sport. Being new, I didn't know a lot of people but I was selected to be on a really good team.

The men's club had a tradition of freshman initiation called "peon day". They would auction off the freshmen who were high school big shots in sports, political office, or award winners.

The rest of the freshmen were assigned to an upper classman. They were each required to wear a beanie throughout the whole day and act as a servant for their master, who was the upper classman.

As I had already attended two colleges and had graduated from high school a year and a half ago, I refused to take part in this ritual. My friend Larry, who was a freshman, took a similar position and refused to wear his beanie or participate.

Some of the upper classmen grabbed him and took him out to a remote area about five miles away. They stripped him down to his underwear, poured molasses all over him, and then covered him with feathers from a pillow. He was then left to make his own way back to campus.

I had no intention of being easy prey. I walked around campus with my favorite baseball bat. Many upper classmen were eyeing me surreptitiously, trying to decide if I would actually use my bat against them. I almost dared them to try to take me as they had taken Larry.

I carried my bat the whole day. I got some catcalls and was heckled here and there, but no one had the courage to try to take me down.

That evening I was walking through campus and I saw two heads behind the large entryway leading to the administration building. I stopped and looked around. I saw no one else. I decided that my friend, Louisville Slugger, and I would be okay.

As I walked closer to the stairway, two more guys came up behind me. I hustled into the stairway with concrete walls on each side.

There were now four of them, all standing in front of me.

"What are you doing with the bat?" they chided.

"Look guys, I'm not a freshman. I graduated two years ago, not last year." I said.

"What are you doing with the bat?" they asked again.

"Look, you guys can probably take me down but I promise you, someone is going to get hurt," I said, trying to reason with them.

One of them lunged toward me and I swung the bat, just missing him. They now knew I was serious and were in a dilemma as to how to proceed. They called me a few names and told me they would get me later, and then they left.

In my history class, I sat by a student named Jerry. He seemed nice enough and was a quarterback on one of the football teams. After one class, he asked if I would like to come up to his room and meet some of his friends.

"Sure," I said.

In the room were Jerry and three others, Bill, Harry, and Bruce. They were talking about a variety of things, especially sports.

"Bill, you've never had a pink belly, well tonight is the night," one of them said suddenly.

The other three jumped on Bill, and when they had finally worn him out, they raised his shirt and took turns slapping him on the belly. His belly turned beet red and he was in obvious pain.

Bill got up, went over to a mirror, and pulled up his shirt to admire his red belly. The others were laughing hysterically.

Then Harry looked at me and said: "You're next."

"That's not going to happen," I said as I stood up.

I turned to leave, and there stood Bruce blocking the door. Bruce was a big guy, probably an inch or two taller than me, and probably outweighed me by 25 pounds.

"Get out of my way," I said.

Instead, he came at me. My judo skills kicked in. I flipped him over my hip and got him in a chokehold. He soon gave up and I let him go. He was coughing and wheezing.

I thought I was coming here to meet some of Jerry's friends, but that was a façade. I was lured here to get my men's club initiation.

We all sat back down and talked. Later we all became good friends. Jerry in particular became one of my closest friends, and was my future roommate.

We are still good friends to this day.

A TRUE MAN OF GOD

I kept checking with dad to see if my car had sold. The answer was always, not yet.

One Sunday afternoon Suzy and I were hanging out in my dorm's lobby. I looked up and saw my mom and dad coming toward us. I was not expecting them and this seemed like a strange situation.

They said they had been visiting some old college friends over the weekend and had come by to see me before they went home.

It wasn't long before the truth came out.

They had indeed sold my car, but had decided *not* to give me any of the money because of the debt I had left them with following my departure from Andrews the year before.

"I promised Mr. Manley that money," I said. "He has been such an advocate and allowed me to get into PUC with the promise that I would give him the money when I sold my car, and I cannot break that promise."

"Sorry," Mom said softly and insincerely.

They got up and walked out to their car. I could see that my dad had a tear in his eye and hated that this was happening. I knew he had no choice in the matter.

I followed mom to their car and said: "You are no longer part of my life, I never want to see you again."

I turned and strode back to the steps to stand beside Suzy.

As I stood there watching them leave, I felt totally liberated. This was a brand new chapter in my life. I was a survivor, and I knew I would make it without them.

I was standing by Suzy, the most wonderful woman I had ever met and the love of my life. I was so thankful for her. She was my partner and soul mate. I felt at peace, and a strange sense of gratification filled my soul.

Now, I had to tell Mr. Manley what had happened.

He told me that he had already contacted my parents about the student loan, and that they had advised him they would not sign for me because of what had happened at Andrews.

"Things are going really well at the gas station. We want you here at PUC so let's forge ahead and see if we can work things out," Mr. Manley said. "You keep up the good work and do well in your classes and I'll help you stay in school."

I couldn't believe what a great guy he was. He was truly sent by God!

A short time later, Suzy's dad, who had worked for Turner's, a moving and storage company in the area, came up with an idea.

He would contact Mr. Turner about the possibility of employment. He thought it might be a better-paying job than working for the school gas station. I decided I would check it out.

The semester was coming to an end, and if I was going to make a job change I needed to hurry so that I could plan my class schedule around it.

I called Turner's and arranged to come in for an interview.

The interview went well and I was offered a job based on Suzy's dad's recommendation. I would be required to work two ten-hour days a week, and receive double my current wage. They gave me a day to ask Mr. Manley for his permission, and to work on my class schedule.

To my surprise, Mr. Manley not only agreed, but thought it would help me immensely.

We worked out an agreement to repay my debt to PUC, and he even said he would talk to the gas station for me.

I remember thinking how lucky I was that Mr. Manley was in my corner. I couldn't believe how everything was finally working out for me. Was God watching over me?

I talked to my advisor and my classes were changed so that I had no Tuesday or Thursday classes.

Grades were due to come out and I was quite nervous. To my surprise, they were pretty good. I was on the road to success, with Suzy by my side supporting me all the way.

Then something happened that threatened everything.

I received a letter from the Selective Service requiring me to come in for a physical. With the Vietnam War well under way, I couldn't imagine myself being inducted.

I talked to Mr. Manley about my concerns. He was so calm and positive.

He looked at my grades and said: "Let's see what I can do. I will attempt to get you a temporary student deferment. With you staying out a year, it may be tough but your grades are good. Let's see how it goes."

He advised me to go for the physical, and plan to come back after Christmas break.

Christmas vacation arrived and Mr. Turner offered me extra work. Each day over the holiday period, Monday to Friday, I was moving books from the old library to a new building at the local university.

This was a godsend, as I didn't know what I was going to do over the holidays. I knew I would not be going home.

The extra income allowed me to make progress on payments to PUC, and hopefully have enough to buy books and supplies for next semester.

The job went really well, and when I presented Mr. Manley with the extra payment, I received one of the best compliments I have ever had.

"Ted, you are going to not only make it, but you will become something special."

This is one of the first times in my life that someone has taken me under their wing and believed in me. I could not let this man down.

"Have you heard anything about my deferment?" I asked.

"Not yet, but I should hear something soon." he replied.

A few weeks later, I had a message to see Mr. Manley.

I knew this was it. Was I going to be inducted? Or had he pulled off another miracle?

When I walked into his office, he couldn't hide his elation. I had my student deferment! I couldn't believe it. I was elated! I gave him a huge hug and thanked him, all the while trying to hold back my tears.

I couldn't wait to tell Suzy.

LIFE CHANGING DAY

*s the year progressed, Jerry and I became good friends. One day he told me that he had talked to his parents and they had come up with a plan for the summer.

I would go to his home and stay with them for the summer, and I would work as an orderly in their family-owned rest home.

Summer came and I stayed with Jerry's family as planned.

It was an added surprised when Jerry and some of his friends invited me to play on their fastpitch softball team.

It was going to be a great summer.

I worked the midnight shift at the rest home, finishing around 7:30 a.m. When I arrived "home" each morning, Queen (Jerry's mom's nickname) would always have breakfast ready.

After breakfast, Jerry went to summer school and I went to bed.

In the afternoon's Jerry and I would often play golf. I had taken a golf class but otherwise had never played. Jerry was my mentor and patiently taught me the finer points. I soon fell in love with the game and we played almost every afternoon.

Jerry had two sisters, Sue and Jane. They were a hoot. We had lots of fun trying to out-trick each other. They usually got the best of me, but I loved it.

Jerry's dad was a doctor and well known in their town. He was the quiet one of the family and always had a beautiful outlook on life.

Queen was a character and I always loved talking to her and getting her perspective on life.

I had never been around such a happy family.

One day Jane and Sue saw an article in the paper about a Cincinnati Reds tryout.

As soon as I woke up, they showed it to me.

Wow! I had to go.

Sue and Jane wanted to go with me, and I was happy for them to come along.

The big day arrived and I was really excited. I had taken the previous night off work so that I could be rested. Although I was excited, I was also really nervous, especially since I had not played any baseball for a year.

When we arrived at the tryout complex, there was a huge crowd and the registration line was quite long. I got in line and eventually registered. My number was 157, which was pinned to my shirt.

I couldn't believe how many players were here, and how they were all decked out in their school uniforms. I had on a pair of cut-off jeans and a white T-shirt.

"How is a person supposed to get noticed with this many participants?" I thought.

I talked to one of the scouts and told him I had to be at work at three o'clock. He said I should be okay.

The leader of the tryouts soon made some announcements.

There were two hundred and forty registered to try out. The eighty pitchers and catchers would be in a different area and would not be required to run in the sprints. The remainder were assigned to areas to warm up.

Soon it was time to start.

There were 13 fifty-yard running lanes painted on the grass, and there would be twelve races. The winner of each race would run again in the finals. As our number was called, we headed to the designated running lane.

My number was called in the fifth race. I could feel my heart pounding and my adrenaline pumping. I bent into a sprinter's starting position, as I had done many times before when I had run track.

Everything was quiet and I concentrated on hearing the starter's gun.

BANG!

The gun went off—and I went blank.

"Congratulations, you will run in lane five in the finals," one of the coaches said to me.

I had won the race!

I walked back to the bleachers and glanced over at Sue and Jane. They were smiling from ear to ear and giving me the big thumbs up.

Soon, all of the preliminary races were run and they asked the winners to take their appropriate lanes for the finals.

I went to lane five.

I was trying to stay calm, but I was really nervous. I glanced in both directions along the line to check out my opponents. Most of them were African Americans and looked like "big time" track athletes. This was really going to be tough. These guys knew what they were doing. I would have to run a perfect race to have a chance.

The starter said: "Gentleman, take your marks, SEEETTT...," and then the starting gun fired.

My start was good, I felt good, and at the finish I leaned forward over the finish line.

One of the scouts came up and congratulated me. Most of my racing competition came up and congratulated me.

I couldn't believe it.

I had won!

Unbelievable!

The scouts then had all outfielders move to right field and throw. We would each get four balls hit to us. The first two balls we would throw to second base, the third ball we would throw to third base, and the fourth ball we would throw to home.

The guy in front of me was quite weak. His throws to second had at least two hops. His throws to third and home barely rolled that distance and were way off line.

I couldn't have been in a better position.

My first two balls were thrown to second with no hop. My throws to third and home had one hop and were right on line.

I felt the throwing segment had really gone well, and I was feeling great.

Then the outfielders were instructed to sit in the bleachers while the infielders went through their drills.

I looked over at Sue and Jane. They were giving me the big thumbs up again. They were hilarious, but with their presence and support it helped relieve some of the pressure I was feeling. They were the sisters I had never had.

The infielder drills took quite awhile. I became concerned that time could become an issue as I needed to be at work by three.

When the infielders were done, the head scout said we would now play a scrimmage game and proceeded to announce the teams.

The first team went to the field and the second team went to the dugout.

I was not selected for either team.

A player from the San Francisco University team came over and invited me to sit with them. They were decked out in their college uniforms and looking pretty sharp.

I thought it was nice of him to invite me to join them, and when I sat down they all introduced themselves.

"I can't believe I didn't get put on a team. I have to go to work soon, and they know this," I said, my disappointment clear.

The player sitting next to me laughed, "Don't worry, they love you. We have been to a lot of tryouts, and if you have speed you go to the head of the line. When the pitcher's position comes up they will probably call you to pinch hit."

Sure enough, that's exactly what happened.

"Number 157, you will bat third in this inning," the head scout announced.

Oh, wow!

That's me!

I couldn't believe it. I was so nervous. I looked at Sue and Jane, and got four thumbs up this time. They were really into this. I had never seen such big smiles. I was really feeding off them.

I grabbed a bat and warmed up, then began watching the pitcher. He threw hard but seemed to have little else. He was from a university in Sacramento.

He struck out the two guys in front of me, maybe he was better than I thought.

Finally, it was my turn. I got in the batter's box and stared at the pitcher. He was a big guy who appeared quite cocky. He wound up and threw a fastball right down the middle.

I froze and just watched it go by.

I stepped out of the box and gave myself a little pep talk. What are you doing, idiot? This is the chance of a lifetime and you just let a perfect pitch go right down the middle. You'll never get that pitch again.

I stepped back into the batter's box with total and intense focus.

The pitcher wound up and threw the same pitch right down the middle—and I hit it over the left center field fence for a homerun.

I ran around the bases in a trance.

I couldn't believe this had just happened.

The head scout called me over to talk.

The questions flowed: Who are you? We don't know you. We know everybody and you are not on our radar. Where do you go to school?

After talking for a few minutes, he said: "I know you need to go to work, but I will be in touch."

The ride back home with Sue and Jane was full of laughter and disbelief. They couldn't wait to get home and tell everyone.

Had this really happened, I kept asking myself.

It was one of the best days of my life! I couldn't wait to tell Suzy. I wish she could have been here.

A few days later, the head scout called and wanted me to play for a semi-pro team that they sponsored.

I ended up playing about ten games with them. Things went well for me on the team, and when it was over the scout offered me a contract.

I told him my parents would not sign so I would have to wait until January 1. I would then be twenty-one and could sign for myself.

He agreed to wait.

For a bunch of college kids, our softball team had done really well that summer. We lost a close game to the best team and finished second.

Our sponsor threw a dinner party for us at the end of the summer. I was hoping Suzy could come but she had no way of getting here. Sue, Jane, Jerry, Doc, and Queen would be my family for the occasion.

When the festivities were over, I was talking to some of my teammates when—I couldn't believe my eyes!

There, at the back of the room, were my parents.

I didn't want to make a scene, but I wasn't happy that they were here. I had not seen or talked to them for ten months.

I went over and my dad gave me a big hug.

"What are you guys doing here?" I asked.

"We were told families were invited so we thought we would come," Dad replied.

A lot had happened since I had last seen them. They didn't know about my new job, my grades, my military physical, my student deferment, or the successful tryout with the Cincinnati Reds.

I decided this was not the time to fill them in.

We spoke for a short time and they told me that Tim had decided to go to PUC. I couldn't believe it; this was great!

I thanked them and told them I had to leave for work.

I know I was not very gracious, but I was not ready to reconcile with them.

TIM AND TED TOGETHER AGAIN

A few days later, Tim and I talked about his plans. I was elated that he was coming to PUC. We were still very close, and now to be reunited again. We could room together, play sports, and generally have a great time.

Tim was chosen on a rival football team in intramurals. Our teams didn't play against each other until the last game of the season, and we were both undefeated.

Final score: Tim's team 22, my team 21.

It was a bitter loss, but all losses are bitter for me.

A few weeks later, Tim and I both made the All-Star team, which would play our rival college in Southern California; La Sierra. Last season we lost the game played on their home ground.

This year we felt good about our chances. I loved that Tim and I would be on the team together.

The day of the game arrived.

The score stayed 0-0 until halfway through the first half.

Then we scored—it was 7-0.

Tim was the defensive back on the right side and I was the defensive back on the left.

On La Sierra's ensuing drive they threw a fairly long pass to Tim's side of the field; that was intercepted by Tim.

He ran straight ahead and then suddenly veered left toward my position, and handed the ball off to me. I ran into the end zone with nobody within ten yards.

We had totally caught them by surprise, and from that point we dominated the game.

Years later at a professional conference, a fellow came up and said he was on the La Sierra team that we had beaten so convincingly.

"When you and your brother pulled that reverse on an interception, it broke our backs and our spirit," he said. "I have never seen that play before or since. I think it's probably something only twins could pull off."

I never told him that Tim and I weren't twins.

Soon after this, the Selective Service System conducted a lottery to determine the order of call to military service. This meant that they would be pulling three hundred and sixty-five capsules, each containing a day of the year. It was speculated that if your birthday coincided within the first one hundred and eighty dates, you would most likely be drafted.

That night when they were conducting the draw, a bunch of us went to the school radio station and watched the ticker tape as it rolled out the dates.

The forty-ninth date was November 23, Tim's birthday. I was sick and heartbroken. Tim seemed to take it in stride, but I knew he was hurting.

My birthday came up at 309. I was home free.

A few days later, I asked Tim how he was doing.

"Well, I don't really like it, but I know God is watching over me. Remember Psalms 91?" he said.

This was one of the Bible chapters that we had memorized as a family.

Tim seemed so strong and grounded in his relationship with the Lord. I wondered what I would be thinking if things had been reversed.

In the spring, Tim had indeed been drafted and left school.

At that same time, I received a letter stating that I should take a break from PUC.

As it turned out, the school officials had learned of some marijuana parties on campus and thought I might have been involved.

Either way, they were cleaning house.

In those days, marijuana use was much more serious and more uncommon than it is today.

I was certainly not a perfect person and had been involved in a lot of pranks, but pot, tobacco, and alcohol were never something I did, if for no other reason than to protect my body so I could be the best baseball player I could be.

I decided to go back to Andrews where Clyde was still in the seminary. It would be fun to be reunited with him.

I talked to Suzy, she talked to her parents, and it was decided that she could go with me.

When we departed from the San Francisco Airport, it was a beautiful 75-degree day. When we arrived in Chicago it was 20 degrees and windy.

We were not dressed for this. The weather was beyond terrible, what have we done?

Clyde was there to meet us, and when we told him we couldn't handle this weather he just laughed and said, "You'll get used to it".

When we arrived at Andrews and began the registration process, a lady asked Suzy and me to follow her to the president's office.

"What are we doing here?" Suzy asked.

"I don't know," I replied.

Soon we were called into his office.

He introduced himself and then said: "I understand you are from PUC."

"Yes, sir," we replied in unison.

"Well, I have one question for you," he said. "Do either one of you smoke marijuana?"

"No, sir," we said.

"Okay, go ahead and register and I hope you have a successful semester."

When we had left the president's office, I said to Suzy: "Word sure gets around fast!"

THE RACE, THE LETTER, AND SAYING GOODBYE

*A*fter registration, Suzy and I went to our dorms.

There I met with an old acquaintance, Everett, who was the dean at Andrews. He said he had just returned from the National Dean's Convention and had met up with the dean of men at PUC.

He'd asked what kind of person I was, and if I smoked pot. The PUC dean told him that he didn't think I did, but that Tim and I had ruffled a few feathers, especially one lady in the P.E. department because we were always playing basketball when the gym was closed for classes.

The PUC dean also told him that I had signed to play baseball with the Cincinnati Reds.

"Don't tell anybody anything about yourself and your baseball abilities," Everett said to me. "I'm a captain in the men's fastpitch intramural league and I want you on my team."

This sounded great.

A day or so later the teams had been chosen. I was waiting for the dean to let me know that I was indeed on his team.

While I was waiting, a guy came up and introduced himself. His name was Dick.

"You are on my fastpitch team," he said.

I wonder how that happened.

"We will have a practice tomorrow," he added.

I must admit I was disappointed.

Later that day I saw the dean. He told me that Dick had a friend at PUC who had told him about me. Dick just managed to pick me before the dean could.

The league was strong and very competitive. Both the dean's team and our team went undefeated, and we met for the last league game of the season.

The dean was a real competitor and a really strong pitcher.

The final score was 6 to 2; we lost.

Then the post-league tournament started and it came down to the dean's team and our team once again.

The final score was 6 to 0; and this time we were the victors.

A few weeks after we had arrived at Andrews, I went down to the weight room. By then there was a buzz around about me being a signee with the Cincinnati Reds.

There was Albert, still doing his thing. He saw me and said hello. Amazing! I didn't think he even knew who I was.

The niceties soon faded and he started chiding me and talking very loudly.

The weight room became quiet as everyone wanted to see this drama unfold.

"You think you're something special just because you play baseball," he said. "I heard you were pretty fast, but there is not a person in this school that is faster than me."

Is this guy for real?

After Tom Smith embarrassed him during my freshman year, I would have thought he might have learned his lesson.

My friend Todd, who was with me, said to Albert: "You don't know who you're dealing with."

Albert would not be deterred.

"Do you think you can beat me in a hundred-yard dash?" he asked.

"You are too big and cumbersome to be any kind of sprinter," I said.

"I might not be an Olympic sprinter, but I will beat you," he boasted.

I snickered and said: "Would you like to put a small wager on it?"

"No," he said, "I would like to put a large wager on it."

"Let's go," I said.

"Not now. I've just worked out and I'm exhausted," he replied.

We set a date and time for the next week.

Could this guy be fast? I knew I was in good shape, and there weren't many people who could beat me in a short sprint.

On the night of the race, hundred-yard lines were marked off in front of the dorm.

Albert showed up just as he said he would. It was a scene like I had never seen before. As I looked down the sidewalk it was lined with students: the word had spread. This had turned out to be a real event.

The starter told each of us his starting cadence, and then he would shoot the starter's pistol. If there was a false start he would shoot the pistol again.

We took our positions.

The starter said: "READY, SEEETTT...," and then the starting gun fired.

I got off to a good start and went as hard as I could.

At about the seventy-five-yard mark I looked around and Albert was about seven or eight yards back. I finished the last ten yards running backwards.

A number of students started ridiculing Albert. I had really wanted to humiliate this puffed up, overbearing, buffoon, but now I felt sorry for him. He walked off totally dejected.

I knew I had not in any way acted like a Christian.

I followed Albert and when I caught up to him, I apologized for my antics.

"My best friend told me I was crazy for challenging you and that as a professional baseball player you almost assuredly could run," Albert explained. "It's a good lesson. My mouth often gets me into trouble."

That spring Suzy and I went to our first hockey game in Chicago and watched the Blackhawks play the Boston Bruins. I couldn't believe the speed, the wild action, and the fights. It was exhilarating.

Having Clyde around again was great. Suzy really didn't know him before and was excited to finally get to know the "nice" brother.

Most of that semester was a lot of fun, however one day Suzy received a letter from her mom.

She read it to herself and then slid it into her pocket. It was obvious that she didn't want to show it to me, but I bugged her until she let me read it.

A friend of Suzy's mom had told her that I wasn't a nice person, and that PUC had kicked me out. She was told that I had gotten into trouble for not going to church and that I had been involved in a number of fights.

Her mom told her that she thought it would be a good idea to keep her options open as far as boyfriends go.

The letter really made me think.

I loved Suzy and couldn't stand the thought of losing her. And I really liked Suzy's mom. I knew she was only trying to protect her daughter, and maybe she had some legitimate concerns.

I talked to God: "I know I'm not a good SDA, but I am a Christian. Does that make me a bad person? Help me, Lord. I can't lose Suzy."

The semester soon ended. Clyde and I took Suzy to Chicago to fly home. I can't believe how tough it was to see her walk away and get on the plane.

Clyde and I were going to San Antonio to see Tim at Fort Sam, where he was in Basic Training.

I had less than a week before I had to be at the Cincinnati Reds spring training camp in Tampa, Florida.

When we arrived at Fort Sam, Tim was thrilled to see us. He got to go out and eat Mexican food (our favorite) and run around a little. The couple of days we were there passed quickly, and I had to catch a flight to Tampa. Clyde, Tim and I all had a special prayer together before I left.

Clyde gave an impassioned plea to God to protect me and my

endeavors, but to especially protect Tim. With the Vietnam War, and Tim to soon be deployed, it was a sobering time.

We knew that, at Fort Sam, out of every eight classes, six went to Vietnam, one went to Germany, and one went to Korea.

We were all hoping and praying that, please God, let Tim go to Germany or Korea.

When Clyde finished praying, we all had tears in our eyes. I gave Tim a big hug, not knowing his future and if or when I would see him again.

I can't believe how tough it had been to say goodbye to Suzy and Tim, the two people in this life that I loved so dearly.

MINOR LEAGUE LIFE

*W*hen I arrived in Tampa, a bus picked up several of us who were arriving for spring training. We were taken to the Reds' complex and allocated a room.

The next morning there was a knock on my door and some of the guys invited me to join them for breakfast.

We went to a little diner and I ordered eggs and hash browns.

"You forgot the bacon," they pointed out.

"No, I don't eat it," I replied. My SDA upbringing is showing already.

Soon my breakfast arrived and there was this white stuff put down in front of me.

"What's this?" I asked.

The guys started laughing.

"Where are you from? California?" they said jokingly. "Those are grits. They come with everything."

I took a spoonful, and they had no taste.

"Put some butter and honey on them," one of them said.

I did, and they were edible—just.

The first day of spring training wasn't too bad, we had a two-hour meeting where they outlined all the rules and regulations.

One item of interest was a list of restaurants and bars we were not allowed to enter. The reason: These were the places Pete Rose had visited and caused trouble.

We all laughed, but I think it might have been at least partially true.

After the meeting, we went through a tough warm up, then threw to each other in an organized drill.

Then came the fifty-yard races.

We were split into three groups: the first and third basemen and catchers; the pitchers; and outfielders and middle infielders.

Then there was an announcement by the coach that there was an assumption that the last group was the fastest group. If anyone in the other two groups thought they were fast enough to join them to let him know.

This blocky-built pitcher volunteered.

The pitchers were the first to race. Some were fairly fast, and others were unbelievably slow.

Then the first and third basemen and catchers ran. I was surprised at how athletic and fast they were.

Then it was my group. I thought back to the tryout camp and the success I had there, could this go as well?

The blocky pitcher was placed a couple of people to my right. On my left was an athletic-looking black player named Ken Griffey. I had heard he was fast.

We took our starting positions and waited for the gun.

BANG!

We were off. I got a good start and so did Griffey. I glanced to my right and the blocky pitcher was ahead of me by about a yard. While I edged out Griffey, the blocky pitcher had beaten us all.

His name was Don Gullett, one of the Reds' top draft choices, and he had been featured in Sports Illustrated. In one high school football game he had scored seventy-one points himself, which included eleven touch downs and five extra points.

The rest of spring training was tough. I thought I was in pretty good shape but this training took it to a whole new level.

95

We had about two grueling weeks of it before assignments would come out. Those that made the top half would go to Sioux Falls, South Dakota, and the bottom half would go to Bradenton, Florida.

During spring training, I was thinking a lot about Tim, hoping and praying he would go anywhere but Vietnam. The stories about that war were horrific. His assignment was almost due. One night, one of the guys called for me to come to the pay phone. It was Tim.

"Ted, I'm going to Korea!" he said.

I broke down and cried. Oh, God, thank you.

When I got off the phone I called Suzy and told her the great news.

Spring training had gone well for me and it was coming to an end.

On the last day, I had heard that it was between me and Griffey as to who was going to Sioux Falls.

We had a scrimmage that day and I had a double, a single, and stole one base. Griffey was hitless, but stole a base after he had walked.

Maybe I got it. Maybe. I was so anxious to hear the results and I knew everyone else was, too.

The next morning we had a meeting to announce the assignments.

The team going to Sioux Falls is…. One name after another….

Come on, read faster….

"Ted Evans" was finally announced.

I jumped with joy. I couldn't believe it.

Soon after, I bought Suzy a watch and asked her to marry me.

The SDAs don't wear rings, so the watch was the customary item given for an engagement.

When she received it, she called and said the watch was beautiful—and said YES!

Immediately after our first game, something happened that was a total surprise to me.

We lost the game and retreated to the locker room to shower and clean up. Two guys who had played and hit well, had a towel fight and were laughing and goofing off.

Really, I thought, we just lost! Why would you be having fun afterward?

Our manager came in and told them to cut it out.

It was a lesson in what minor league baseball is all about. Your number one priority is not how the team does, but how "I" do. If someone gets hurt and it gives me an opportunity to play or move up, that's great. I quickly learned that it is the most selfish world I had ever experienced.

Another thing that became obvious is that most minor league baseball players are focused on two things, chasing women and drinking.

If we had a day game, most of the guys would go out drinking afterwards, staying at the bar until all hours of the night. They would often ask me to go with them, and I would tell them I don't drink.

"Why not?" they'd ask.

"Because I never have, and because I don't want to waste an opportunity by throwing it away in a bar," was my reply.

The nights after a day game, I would play ping-pong or pool at the complex. The whole thing really got old. I spent a huge amount of time and money on phone calls to Suzy. I felt so all alone. That was one of the longest summers I had ever experienced.

Once the league was over, I couldn't wait to get home and see Suzy.

Before we could leave, we had an evaluation meeting with the manager and a member of the Reds' scouting program. They offered me a contract for the following year and told me how much potential I had.

I told them how miserable I had been, and that I would be getting married next spring.

"That's great," they said. "You will be much happier with a wife to go home to."

I looked at the contract; there was a nice raise included.

I decided to sign.

DID I MAKE THE RIGHT DECISION?

*O*n my way home I was already regretting re-signing. I had dreamed of playing professional baseball my entire life, and when I got the chance, it was the most miserable experience of my life. Playing baseball had gone from a great game to total drudgery.

I couldn't wait to get home and discuss it with Suzy. She always seemed to have a good perspective on things.

As we talked, she said things like: This is what you wanted your entire life; Next year I will be with you and we'll have fun; You only get chances like this once, if you walk away you'll always wonder if you could have made it.

Clyde was home for Thanksgiving, as were Suzy and I.

We had already announced our engagement in Suzy's hometown, and would now announce it in mine.

I talked to Clyde about re-signing with the Reds. I told him about my experiences and reservations about going back.

"Do you think I made the right decision?" I asked.

Clyde liked to tell stories to make a point.

"There is a place in Africa where they catch monkeys in an unusual way," he began. "The natives take a gourd, fill it with nuts and goodies that monkeys like, and they anchor it into the ground.

They then hide in the brush. The gourds have a small neck that the monkey can slide its hand down and into the gourd where the goodies are, but when it grabs a handful of those goodies, it cannot pull its hand back out of the gourd. The natives come running with their net and snag the monkey, who will not let go of its catch.

"You have said to me on several occasions that professional baseball is not a Christian environment," he went on to say. "You have in fact said it is the most selfish, self-centered environment you have ever seen. In this life, there are givers and takers. If you are a taker there is never enough, and if you are a giver you will always have satisfaction.

"I believe God has a plan for you. Your talents are not just for playing baseball. You have a lot to give and God would use your talents, or you can pursue fame and fortune, but I'm sure you will never be satisfied in that pursuit. If you choose God and his plan, you must be different than the African monkeys and let go."

Why did Clyde always make so much sense?

Suzy and I spent many hours debating the pros and cons of returning for my second year. We finally decided to just sit on it for a while. I don't know why we didn't just decide. We knew what the right thing to do was. I guess I had some monkey in me.

I had reapplied and been accepted back into PUC for my junior year, and Jerry would be my new roommate. When I returned from playing baseball, Suzy and I bought a VW Bug. It made everything so much easier.

One weekend we went to her home for the weekend.

On Sunday evening, on our way back to PUC, there was an announcement over the radio. Two PUC students had been attacked at a nearby lake.

Cecelia Shepard (CC) and Bryan Hartnell were stabbed numerous times and both were in critical condition at the local hospital. Police believe it may have been the Zodiac killer.

The campus was buzzing with the news. I couldn't believe this. Bryan Hartnell lived on my hall in the dorm. Everyone was pretty freaked out. For the next two days we all had prayer vigils for Bryan and CC.

Unfortunately, CC passed away two days after the attack. Her funeral was one of the saddest I have ever attended. She was so young and had a great future.

The whole campus was devastated. Many questioned how God could have let this happen to such good people. It was so unfair.

Bryan, after some difficult days, made progress and eventually regained his health and continued school at PUC. We were all grateful that Bryan had made it.

You could not have been at PUC that year without having some somber memories.

They never caught the Zodiac killer.

The rest of that year flew by.

Suzy and I were getting married right after school ended and just before spring training. I was still not sure it was the right thing to do, but that was our plan at that moment.

The following year we were going to go back to Andrews. In the SDA school system, Andrews was considered to have the top Physical Education program. I thought it would be good for me to graduate from there.

As school and my junior year at PUC was coming to an end, the decision on playing minor league ball was looming large. I hated to burden Suzy with this when she was busy planning our wedding, so I decided just to go on back to spring training and see how things went.

The wedding went off without a hitch, and we spent a couple of days in San Francisco.

Then I was off to Tampa for spring training.

It was much more comfortable at Tampa this time around. However, as time went on and spring training was ending, I got a strange feeling.

Is this what God wants me to do?

I seriously doubt it. How could he want me in an occupation where all I was doing was pursuing such selfish ambitions? Was I a better person, helping people, giving more, and glorifying God more, if I played baseball? Was I less proud and unselfish when I was playing baseball? That's a laugh.

The truth is; I could tell I had lost much of my desire to play. I knew it would be much better when Suzy could be with me, but I also knew that there would be no chance I would make the majors without an extreme amount of desire and dedication.

I called Suzy and told her my thoughts.

"What do you think?" I asked her.

"I'd hate to have you quit and regret it," she said, "but I'm with you all the way whatever you decide."

Then an idea hit me like a bolt.

"Suzy, I have an idea," I said. "Our assignments are coming out in a couple of days. It's time to put God to the test. I'm going to put out Gideon's fleece. If I'm assigned to Sioux Falls, we will stay and play. If I am assigned anywhere else, we are throwing in the towel."

"Good plan, let's do it," she said.

Two days later the assignments were given out. I was assigned to Tampa.

I called Suzy and said the answer has been given. I'm done.

I went to the Reds' manager in charge of spring training and told him. He said Chief Bendor, the head of the Reds' minor league system, would be here in a couple of days. He would have to release me since I had signed a contract. When Chief Bendor arrived, we all sat down and discussed my situation.

Mr. Bendor was really nice and very professional. He laid out a plan for me to reach the major league team.

"Speed is a top priority for our prospects," he said. "You have that, however you are lacking in experience. With your abilities, your path can be accelerated with just plain hard work. You have the potential and we want you in the system."

He looked at me for a response. I kept thinking as he was talking. I had put God to the test and I believe he answered me. Is there any way I should go against the test.

"Mr. Bendor, I really appreciate you taking the time to meet with me, and I also really appreciate your complimentary remarks about my abilities and potential," I said. "However, there is one huge problem. I don't think I have a chance to make it to the majors without desire, and I have lost the desire to play. I believe God has a different plan for my life."

Mr. Bendor sat there looking at me, like: Is this guy nuts?

"You are absolutely right," he said. "No one has ever made it without desire. It is a tough road even with it. I appreciate your candor and I will sign a release for you."

I have often been asked if I have any regrets about quitting. The answer is no. But sometimes I wonder if I would have made it to the majors, especially as a couple of players that I had played ahead of, had made it.

SENIOR YEAR AND FIRST JOB

*S*uzy and I arrived at Andrews University in August for our senior year.

Dean Everett had helped us find a house near campus and had gotten me a good job as a student intramural director.

I couldn't believe that so many things had been taken care of for us before we had even arrived.

Dean Everett was really a good friend.

We both knew exactly what classes we needed to finish. My classes would be almost all P.E., and Suzy's would be all speech pathology classes.

Our finances were all in order and we were really excited about our senior year and our new life together.

Registration day came and Suzy and I went our separate ways to be advised and registered. Everything went like clockwork for me and I sat around and waited for Suzy.

Finally, she showed up. She had a strange look on her face.

"Ted, the speech pathology department is closing down," she said.

"Are you kidding me?" I said. "What happened?"

"The rumor is that the man in charge of the program has run off with his secretary," she said.

"What do we do now?" I asked.

As we considered our options, I suggested we go back to PUC. Suzy was adamant that we needed to stay. P.E. students that graduated from Andrews usually had better job opportunities.

I couldn't believe it. Everything was going so perfectly. There was some talk that the speech pathology program would be up and running again by the second quarter.

That was good news, so we decided to stay.

Suzy took some classes that would still count toward graduation in hopes the program would be resurrected.

At the end of the first quarter, we drove to California for Christmas vacation.

When we returned to Andrews, we found out that the speech pathology program wasn't going to be continued.

If we had known, we might have stayed in California and returned to PUC.

Suzy decided to go to work full time and pick up her last semester later.

The school year was really going well for me, except that as a senior I was nervous about job possibilities. I had talked to a couple of different schools about P.E. jobs and there was one in New York City.

I knew a student who had attended that school and asked him about it.

He said the school was right in the city and it was a good school, but don't take your car there.

We decided to keep looking.

A short time later a school representative from North Carolina talked to me about going to Fletcher Academy.

It was a self-supporting boarding school as it wasn't an official member of any larger organization.

He asked if I had any music experience, especially band. I told him I had played in a band in high school.

"Would you be willing to teach band along with your P.E. classes and Assistant Dean of Boys' duties?" he asked.

"Oh wow, I don't know," I said. "Let me think about that one."

A few days later he called me with a new proposal.

"If you will take the band responsibilities," he said, "we will pay for your schooling between now and graduation, but we would require you to get a minor in music."

There weren't a lot of P.E. job openings and I didn't want to go to New York. I said I would take a trip down there to have a look at the school.

Dean Everett went with me during spring break. We were also going to meet our friend Reed to play some golf as he lived nearby.

We drove to the school in my Corvette.

When we arrived at Fletcher Academy, we met the CEO of the high school and the hospital associated with it.

"Nice jitney you're driving," he said. "I'll bet it will really go."

"Yes, it will," I said.

"Driving over the speed limit is illegal and a crime, you know," he said.

I didn't know how to respond so I kept quiet. Not my best trait.

I don't remember anything else he said because I was too busy thinking what a whacko he was, and what does jitney mean anyway.

Is everyone else around here like him?

As it turned out, I accepted the job and began the arduous task of taking a bunch of music classes. I needed them all to graduate.

One of the classes was piano, taught by a meticulous, demanding oriental lady. She wanted me to practice at least one hour a day.

Dean Everett, Reed, and I were playing golf every chance we had.

One hour a day for piano? There was no time for that.

Every time I went in for my lesson, I was scolded. I kept telling her I was trying, but that I was just no good at it. She would give me a stern look over her glasses and then proceed with the lesson.

Finally, the summer session was over. No more music classes.

At graduation I got in line, all decked out in my cap and gown. It was a Friday night.

Then I saw a very scary sight.

Administrators were coming through the line and pulling some students out. I wondered if I would be one of them.

105

Had my piano teacher failed me? Please just give me a "D", I prayed.

When they came to me, they kept on going. I sighed with relief.

She had given me a "B". What a gift. I think she must have felt sorry for me.

Suzy and I were packed up and ready to go. As soon as the Sunday graduation was over, we were on our way to North Carolina and my first real job.

The next year went really well.

The biggest hurdle in the beginning was the difficulty of understanding these Southerners.

One of my best friends was a teacher named Roger. I couldn't understand half the things he said. For instance, he told me he was going to pick up some "tars". I finally figured that he meant tires.

For many of the other things he said, I just shook my head as if I understood. He was a great guy and we are still friends to this day.

The school had never had any kind of athletic program, even intramurals, which had now become accepted in most SDA schools. I talked to Gordon, the principal, about starting an intramural program.

"Only if I can play," he said.

Gordon was really a good guy.

We started with flag football, and had a faculty team.

Gordon was our center, and he always played with a smile on his face. He had told me that he didn't run very well, but if I threw him the ball he would never drop it. He was right on both accounts.

The kids were loving the intramural program.

Every Monday I posted stats and they would crowd around as I put them on the bulletin board. It was a good feeling to see how happy sports made them feel.

After the first semester, Gordon called me in.

"We have a situation that I have never seen before," he began.

I could see that he had the grades of two boys in front of him.

"Boy number one has straight A's except for an "F" in P.E.," he continued. "Boy number two has straight F's except for an "A" in P.E. I know I'm going to hear about this from their parents.

"You may be on the hot seat with one set of parents and on the good seat with the other's parents. Would you like to tell me about the boy who got the "F" in your class?"

"Yes. He is a boy that hates P.E.," I explained. "I have talked to him on many occasions. He doesn't think he should have to take P.E. I told him it's required, and if he would come to class and try, I would give him a "C". He refused, so I felt I had no choice."

"The only thing I ask is, if something like this happens again, I should be informed," he said.

"The other boy loves sports and P.E.," I added. "I didn't know he was doing so badly in his other classes."

"That, I have no problem with," he said. "The other teachers should have communicated with me about his lack of progress."

Toward the end of the year, I received a call from the principal of Thunderbird Academy in Arizona. He was in the area and wanted to talk.

His name was Don and he was looking for a dean, a P.E. teacher, and an intramural director for the boys at the academy—all positions to be filled by the one person.

He offered me the position.

Soon Suzy and I would begin paying for student loans and we had no idea how we could do that with what we were earning at Fletcher Academy.

My salary at Thunderbird would be almost four times more, and they were going to make our student loan payments as well; both Suzy's and mine.

We had enjoyed our year in North Carolina, but felt we really didn't have much choice but to move. We said several times over the next twenty-four hours how amazing it was that God was opening so many doors for us.

The next day we called Don and accepted the position.

The CEO of Fletcher called me into his office a few days later.

He was very upset.

"We paid your fees for your last semester and this is how you show your appreciation," he said. "You owe us that amount."

"Really?" I said. "I would have had my teaching certification, but I took all of those music classes for you. They are useless to me now."

The CEO continued to rant and told me he would get his money.

I got up and left while he was still raging.

I immediately called Don and told him about the meeting. He laughed and told me not to worry about it; he would take care of it.

I never heard any more about it.

SCOTTSDALE, ARIZONA

*bout a month later we were on our way to Scottsdale, Arizona.

Scottsdale was totally different than North Carolina; it was brown and hot. I loved it, but Suzy wasn't so sure. Hot weather wasn't really her thing.

Don called a meeting with me and the dean of girls. He asked me to come in early to go over a number of my responsibilities. He was well-organized and thorough. I really liked him.

He explained that last year they had two deans, one for boys and one for girls, and a P.E. teacher. Now there would only be the two of us. The girl's dean had agreed to take on the girl's P.E. and intramurals and remain the girl's dean.

"Have you met her yet?" he asked.

"No," I replied.

"She will be here shortly. Her name is Bev," he said. "Then we will go over the summer schedule and how things will work with the reorganization."

All of a sudden, Bev burst into the office and blew right by me. She was grumbling about a student she had seen outside.

I stood when she came in and I'm now thinking, nice to meet you, too.

"What is Jim doing here?" she demanded.

"He's working in the furniture factory this summer," the principal said calmly.

However, she just kept lamenting on how deplorable it was that Jim was on campus.

I walked over to the window to get a look at this Jim monster. He didn't look too scary to me; hair a little long maybe, but otherwise not too scary.

Don was finally able to introduce us. She looked me over and didn't appear too impressed.

Don briefed us on the summer schedule and our responsibilities. Then he went over the calendar for the school year and our responsibilities in P.E. and intramurals.

"I'm not doing intramurals," Bev said defiantly.

This seemed to catch Don off guard. He appeared embarrassed and uncomfortable, and stared at her in silence.

This is interesting, I thought. Who's going to win this dispute?

"Ted's been trained to do intramurals," Bev said. "I haven't, it doesn't make sense that it should be forced on me."

"Bev," Don said, "we have been over this. You have agreed to the job as described. Do you want the job or not?"

"Yes, I want the job, but I don't think it's fair," she said.

"Okay," he said. "Then you know what your new job description is. You have chosen to take the job as described. I don't want to hear about this again unless you don't want to continue."

All right! Don put her in her place nicely. I discovered that day, that a good Christian man could also be tough when needed and do it in a Christian way.

"I'm going to step out," Don said. "You two talk about the summer schedule, who's going to handle what, and I'll be back in a few minutes."

"Instead of us splitting up days to have worship and recreation," Bev began, "why don't we split it up by weeks."

"That's fine with me," I said.

"Okay, you take the first week, and we'll alternate from there," she said.

The first week went well. I was anxious to get to know Jim. He was into basketball and we played some at recreation. My first impression was that he seemed like a good guy. I wondered why Bev portrayed him as such a bad person.

Week two: Suzy and I were having supper in our apartment, which was located in the dorm, when there was a knock on the door. I answered and there stood about twenty-five students.

"What's going on?" I asked.

"We came to see what we're doing for recreation," one of them answered.

"Bev is in charge this week," I said.

"She said you were in charge of recreation, she was just in charge of worship."

I didn't want to make a scene so I sent them to the gym and told them I would be there in five minutes.

The first thing the next morning I talked to Don about the recreation situation.

He was livid.

This began a two-year roller coaster ride where Bev continually tried to bail on her responsibilities and dump them on me. I felt sorry for some of the female students who really wanted to be involved in intramurals and meaningful physical education classes. I finally told Don that I would do some of her P.E. classes. He tried to hold her accountable, but I know this was a constant battle.

It soon became evident that Jim wasn't a monster. He was in fact one of the best athletes at Thunderbird. We became friends within a couple of weeks.

Over summer I came to trust him more and more. I found him to be responsible and respectful. At the end of summer I asked him to be one of my student resident assistants.

Years later, we remain friends.

A few weeks after school started, things seemed to have settled down and were going quite smoothly.

Then one night, two seniors came into my office. They were unhappy about the way I had organized my student staff.

Last year, they explained, they had status and were in student leadership positions. This year, the student staff were mostly athletes who had been in trouble the year before. I felt sorry for them, but I had filled the student staff positions. Fortunately, they had both secured jobs elsewhere on campus.

A lesson learned, I thought. I should have checked this situation out before I hired the current staff.

The next two years went well. Don and I had become friends and we often played tennis. Toward the end of my second year, Everett, my old friend from Andrews, had accepted an offer to be the men's dean at Southern Adventist University, in Collegedale, Tennessee. He asked me if I would go with him and be his assistant.

This was a tough decision. I had fallen in love with Arizona: the weather, the Mexican food, the golf courses, and the kids at Thunderbird. I could hardly see myself leaving.

Suzy and I contemplated the situation. How often would I get a chance like this, especially with my good friend Everett.

The president of the Arizona SDA conference heard about the offer and called a meeting with me and Don. Suzy and I decided it was time to put out Gideon's fleece.

"If the president says to me, Ted we really appreciate your contribution to Thunderbird and we really want you to stay, then we will stay," I said to Suzy. "But if he seems noncommittal then we will pack up and head to Tennessee."

Suzy was totally on board.

I walked into the meeting and the president, who I hardly knew, stood and shook my hand like a haughty politician.

I sat down. He seemed irritated.

"I understand you have an offer to go to Southern," he said. "I need you to make up your mind so we can move forward."

I stood up and said: "Thank you, I just did. I'm out of here."

I walked out without another word.

Don and I talked later.

"I loved how you handled that," Don said. "The president was flabbergasted."

"Don," I said, "I was setting out the fleece and I believed that God was directing my life."

Shortly after I had told the president I was leaving, a few senior students came to me and asked if I would look into a matter.

I was the seniors' sponsor and they had learned that the juniors were going to do something totally new on seniors' night than what was tradition.

The sponsors for the juniors were Bev and her husband.

I went to their apartment that evening and expressed the concern of our seniors about the change to seniors' night.

Bev and her husband said the presentation was at the discretion of the juniors and they could do whatever they wanted. I told them I didn't believe that was true and I was going to research it further.

I got ahold of Don and explained the situation. He was not happy and said he would talk to them and get back to me.

It didn't take long before I got a call from Don. He said they are not allowed to change the presentation protocol, and he had instructed them to stay with the accepted traditions.

There were some juniors that I had a great relationship with who told me they had had a meeting, and because I had raised such a stink, they couldn't make the presentation they had chosen. They also told me that something was being planned to get even. I thanked them.

The presentation was only a week away, on Saturday night.

The seniors' gift to the school was new glass basketball backboards. Printed in the box over the rims was the year of the graduating seniors. These installed during the week before the presentation, and the glass backboards were wrapped so they would not be seen until Saturday night.

On Friday night, I got to thinking; Bev has a key to the gym.

I went to bed and set my alarm for 4:00 a.m. I got dressed and went over to the gym, got up on a ladder, and unwrapped the backboards.

Sure enough, they had changed the year from that of the seniors to that of the juniors. I changed it back and marked the wrappings so I could tell if they were tampered with. On Saturday, I checked my markings and they had not been altered.

When it came time for the presentation, I kept my eye on the junior's sponsors. As the wrappings came off and the correct year was revealed, their haughty smirks turned into looks of dismay as they realized they had been caught. Bev was "seeing red."

Right after graduation, a moving van picked up our furniture and we were headed for Collegedale, Tennessee.

SOFTBALL AND RESIDENCE HALL DON'T MIX

After the three-day journey, we arrived at the campus of Southern Adventist University. Waiting for us was Everett and his wife, Sharon, and Warren and his wife, Judy. Warren was the other assistant dean.

Within a few days the moving van had unloaded our furniture and we were pretty well settled. We were thrilled to be here, it seemed so comfortable.

Warren and Everett told me that there was a Collegedale men's fastpitch team that played in nearby Chattanooga. Warren, who was about six foot three and very athletic, played for the team. He had also played minor league ball for several years in the Philadelphia Phillies Farm System. He was a great guy with a great sense of humor and we hit it off immediately.

We all went down to watch the team play. The caliber of play was phenomenal, I couldn't believe it. Unbeknown to me, Chattanooga was a real hotbed for both men's and women's fastpitch. I had expected a much lower class of play, but wow, these guys were good. They played in the renowned Dixie Major League. Unfortunately, the Collegedale team was in last place.

The manager of the Collegedale team asked me if I would like to play. Absolutely was my immediate reply.

For the next two years the team struggled to get out of the basement and the manager decided to quit. I volunteered to take over the managerial role and my offer was accepted. As it turned out, I both managed and played for the next seventeen years.

Three years after I started managing the team, we brought in a new pitcher, Nelson. He was young but he had a real fire in his belly and, like me, he hated to lose. He was already better than anyone we had ever had, so the sky was the limit on his potential.

That year we won the league. This seemed like a miracle.

The next year a new teacher in the P.E. department also joined our team. He was a great athlete and could virtually play any position, except pitcher. His name was Steve. He soon became the assistant coach and one of my best friends.

Meanwhile back at Southern, my first year of five as an assistant dean went well. Everett, Warren and I had a great relationship and the residence hall program was doing great.

I was making friends with a lot of the guys, especially those who played in intramurals and golf.

There was not currently a school golf tournament, so I decided to start one. The tournament was small, with only five teams.

Oh well, I thought, we have to start somewhere.

On one of the holes, I teed off and hit an excellent drive right down the middle. It hit some hard pan and rolled into the group in front of us.

This one guy in the group took out his driver, teed up my ball, and blasted it right back at me.

Later I found out he was a good golfer and somewhat of a hot head. His name was John. I later contacted John and we talked about things, including what had happened on the course.

John became one of my favorite students, not because he played golf, but I think because he reminded me of myself.

A couple of years later Warren and I were playing tennis and we heard someone hollering. John was walking briskly away from the soccer field and another guy was screaming at him.

John was a senior and had accepted a job in Virginia. We knew John had been in a few altercations and had a reputation as having a short fuse. Warren and I started saying over and over to ourselves: "Keep walking John, keep walking".

Then John's heckler caught up to him, grabbed him by the shoulder, and turned him around. John, without flinching, threw a punch that floored his attacker. We were hoping this would not have any negative effects on his job in Virginia. As it turned out, it didn't.

John's younger brother Matt came to school after John had graduated. I introduced myself and told him I had heard he was a great golfer. Matt and I went on to play a lot of golf together, and entered quite a few tournaments.

When I became Head Dean, I was able to hire Matt as the dean in charge of freshman retention.

Matt and John became lifelong confidants and I consider them more like brothers than friends. I have, on various occasions, used both as consultants, and both have been steady influencers who have had a calming effect on my life.

At the end of my fifth year as assistant dean, Everett and Warren both decided to take different positions. Everett moved from dean of men to dean of students. Warren took a position in one of our sister schools in Southern California.

I wasn't sure what was going to happen to me. I had been an assistant with Everett for five years and I was really hoping to be promoted to Head Men's Dean. I knew I didn't have the ideal amount of experience for the position, but I also knew that Everett had a lot of confidence in me.

A few weeks had passed when Everett came into my office and shut the door.

"You got it," he said.

I was thrilled and scared at the same time. This was an awesome responsibility.

Now it was my turn to find two replacements, one for Warren and one for the position I had vacated. I knew that one of my assistants must have a good sense of humor, like Warren. This might be hard to find. Warren was a class act and really got along well with everyone.

The other assistant I wanted to be more of an academic person, to give the men in our dorm a variety of options.

While I was going through the process of evaluating applicants' resumes, I ran across one that looked familiar. He had been my dean in high school and he pretty much had no use for me. I had been in so much trouble that I couldn't really blame him, now that I looked back.

A day or two later I received a phone call and, low and behold, it was my old high school dean.

"I have looked at your resume," I said. "Pretty impressive. Do you remember me?"

"Can't say that I do," he responded.

"Go back and have a look at the school annual, then call me back," I said.

I never heard from him.

A couple of weeks later, I invited old friends, Ron and Reed, to join me. I knew I would be comfortable with them.

That school year was a real nail biter for me. I really wanted things to go well and I think I was watching everything like an old mother hen. While I wanted the position, I didn't realize how much pressure was attached to it.

Three things had changed drastically from being an assistant to being the head dean.

The first: I was now responsible for everything that happened in the dorm. It all stopped at my desk. The second: I was responsible for keeping all of the staff and student staff happy. And third: I had to represent the dorm on every committee on campus. It seemed like I was in committee meetings all day, every day.

As for the softball team, we continued to improve and dominate. The better we got the more press we got from the Chattanooga media.

One sequence of events really put us on the map.

Our team won seventy-four games in a row, then lost one, and then went on another winning streak of twenty-seven games.

We had won one hundred and one games and lost only one during that streak.

The Chattanooga sports fans started following us during this span and, of course, so did the media. During our winning streak I had two good years and was awarded the Softball Player Of The Year, each of those years by the Old Timer's Club of Chattanooga.

After I had received the second player of the year, the president came by my office. He told me that some were concerned about my involvement in the softball league, and the message it was sending.

We talked about it and he was very respectful and professional. I told him I would attempt to keep my name out of the papers as much as possible.

The president was really coming under attack for a variety of religious positions he had taken. Under the circumstances, I thought he handled things with me very well. However, I began to wonder about my position, and how many SDAs were so judgmental and legalistic.

A group of individuals continued to attack him with written articles about his alleged hypocrisy. I was called into his office, along with other department heads. He had acquired an injunction against his accusers and instructed us that these people were not allowed to be on any part of our campus.

A few days later, I received a phone call at about three in the morning. It was my front desk monitor telling me that there was a man putting papers under the door of every dorm room. I went into the dorm and looked around, but he was gone. The monitor and I went through the dorm, collected the flyers, and took them to my office.

The next morning, my assistant Reed and I were talking about the situation.

Suddenly a large man, probably six foot five and weighing around 280 pounds, stormed into my office. He was the nocturnal mailman, and the papers he had delivered were sitting in a stack on the corner of my desk.

He leaned over, put his hands on the front of my desk, and went berserk, condemning and berating me for picking up his private property.

He was spitting mad and growling like an old bear.

All the while I was wondering what I was going to do if things got physical as he was between the exit and me. Meantime, the longer he lashed out at me, the madder I got.

I had let him go on without saying a word. He finally seemed to be running out of gas and ended his tirade by pointing a finger at me, saying: "If you ever throw away any papers of mine again, you better know karate."

That was the last straw.

I jumped up, grabbed the stack of papers, put them over my head, and threw them into the trash can.

Reed jumped up on the couch.

The big man looked at me as if he had just seen a ghost and had no idea what to do.

I walked up to him and told him to get out of my office, he was trespassing on private property and I was going to call the cops. He turned without a word and briskly walked out.

Later that day the president called and thanked me for my actions.

"What would you have done if he had attacked you?" he asked.

"That man has never been in a fight in his life," I said. "He was big enough that he could intimidate people with his size, but the longer he talked, the more I could see it in his eyes. He was nothing but hot air and I think he realized I was not intimidated. But if he had indeed attacked me, I had a plan, I had Reed."

The president laughed and thanked me again.

I was on very good terms with the president after that.

A year or so later the president resigned.

DOG TROUBLE

⤫

The new president was a very conservative man.

About that time, Suzy and I purchased two Bloodhound puppies.

The first was a male we found in Maryland when we were visiting Clyde. We hadn't had him very long when we decided he needed a playmate. We located a breeder in Dothan, Alabama, who only had one puppy left and it was her prize female. She asked if we would be willing to show her. I told her we were SDA and couldn't show her on Saturdays. She said she would sell us the puppy on a co-own basis. This meant that as the co-owner she would be able to show the dog on Saturdays. We agreed, and named the new puppy, "Brandy".

A couple of years later, Brandy's co-owners where coming from Alabama to attend the Chattanooga Dog Show and we invited them to stay with us on Friday night.

We waited and waited for them, and finally received a phone call to say their vehicle had broken down. Although the car was now repaired, they were still two or three hours away. They decided to stay there and leave early the next morning. They asked if we could bring Brandy to the show site. We said we could.

After the show, we said goodbye to our friends and brought Brandy back home.

A few days later the president called me in to talk about me showing the Bloodhound on Sabbath. I told him what had happened.

"What would you do if a student wanted to go to the dog show on Sabbath?" he asked.

"I would not have a problem with that anymore than if he was going to the zoo," I replied.

"Would you let him skip church to go?" he asked.

"I would probably suggest he wait until afterward," I said.

"You skipped church to go," he pointed out.

Here we go, the old going-to-church law was going to be laid on me. To skip church was, after all, the unpardonable sin.

Everett told me later that the president wanted to fire me. He had told Everett that lots of people were watching to see if he did the right thing. To the legalistic, judgmental conservatives, the right thing no doubt would be to fire me.

Everett said he had appealed to the president; that this was an ox in the pit situation. The president agreed to let me talk to the dorm students at worship and explain what had happened. If that went well he would allow me to stay.

I asked God to help me with my presentation as I suspected the president would be there.

Everett and the president were indeed there.

The chapel was packed.

Although I was nervous, I felt that it went well; and when it ended, the students gave me a nice ovation.

The president seemed impressed and agreed to let me stay.

This current president seemed so conservative; to think he would have fired me over something as ridiculous as the dog show situation.

I was about ready to get out of this school.

I had decided to do the Lord's calling after I had left professional baseball. I wanted to be a Christian, but I was beginning to think that I had made a mistake getting back into the SDA church.

If I decided to stay, I felt the president would watch me like a hawk, and it wouldn't take much to send me packing.

I was still managing the men's fastpitch team. Could that be a reason for him to let me go?

A few months later, there was a shake up in the P.E. department. As a result, there was an opening that, by its description, was perfect for me.

I had my master's degree in P.E. and my teaching certification. Two of the instructors were good friends of mine; Bob, who was the new department chairman, and Steve, who was the intramural coordinator, and also the assistant on our fastpitch team.

This might be the very thing that I needed to resurrect my career at Southern.

I talked to Bob about the possibility of transferring to his department and he seemed very receptive. He told me to apply and go through the process.

Suzy kept saying that the right doors had always opened for us at the right time. I can't imagine this will be any different.

A couple of weeks later Bob hand-delivered a letter and an official invitation to join his team. I was thrilled.

I immediately talked to Everett and got his blessing.

It is amazing how this had all worked out at the very time that I needed it to, just as Suzy had predicted.

A short time later, Reed was announced as the new head dean. I was tickled for him and knew he would do a great job.

A few days later, Bob came by.

"I need to talk to you," he said.

He had a serious look on his face and I immediately became almost panicky. Had the president become involved and nixed the whole transition?

Bob and I went into my office.

"Ted, the job is still yours but the job description has changed," he said.

I was relieved and couldn't figure out what could be the big deal.

"You must be in charge of the gymnastics team," he added.

I sat there almost in shock.

Gymnastics had never been my thing. Would I be miserable trying to coach something I knew very little about?

I asked Bob to give me a little time to contemplate this situation.

My buddy Steve came to see me almost immediately.

"Ted, I will help you with the team," Steve said. "You are a natural coach and can do this."

My dad told me once that a good coach can coach almost anything.

I was told that the former gymnastics coach did not want me to join the department. He was refusing to coach the team and hoped this might be a way of forcing me to turn down the job.

To me, the former coach was throwing down a challenge, and I decided to take that challenge. I told Bob I would accept the job.

I knew the gymnastic job was going to be tough, but I didn't realize how tough it was really going to be.

That summer I called every high school senior gymnast in the SDA schools of the Southeastern United States. There were about thirty-five in all.

One of the very first seniors I talked to woke me up to a grim reality.

"I don't want to be rude," he said, "but the Southern gymnastic team is not as good as our high school team. I am going to go to Andrews, which has the best team."

Over the next month I contacted every one of the gymnastic seniors, and the results were sobering.

Ten were going to Michigan to try out for the team at Andrews. Two were coming to Southern and were going to try out for our team. The rest said they were finished with gymnastics.

This was way beyond disappointing; I felt devastated. To say that I do not like to lose is a major understatement.

Under my management the men's fastpitch team had gone from last to first.

I didn't know how long it would take, but I was confident I could do the same thing with this gymnastic program.

GROWING PAINS

*T*hat fall we had twenty-three students on the team, and only a few were new.

First semester was a laborious process, with many feeling we were practicing too long.

In previous years, practice was mostly voluntary and the focus was on individual routines, which were primarily done on Olympic-style apparatus.

Each member was told that when they thought they had a routine that was show-worthy, it would be evaluated by the coach. If he thought it was good enough, he would allow it to go in the program.

My focus was on team routines and practice was a requirement.

It was soon evident that the students from last year's team were divided as to whether the new philosophy was good or bad. I began hearing that many were not coming back for the second semester.

If the rumors were true, it looked like we were losing about 40 percent of the team.

When the second semester commenced, we had not lost as many as expected, and those we did lose were not as critical to our success as those who stayed. The last program of the year was the Homeshow on our own campus.

It went surprisingly well and I thought we had taken the first step in becoming something special.

In the second year, we had a few more people try out and we gained some new talent. I was pretty excited.

Unfortunately, some of the old team members didn't seem to have much enthusiasm. Right before Christmas break many of the older members came in and told me they were quitting.

I was dejected . I had envisioned our team being much better by now.

When the team returned from Christmas break, rumors were going around that I was going to quit. Two freshman girls came into my office.

"Coach Evans," one said, "you are not going to quit, are you?"

"I don't know," I replied honestly.

"We came to Southern because we really liked what we saw your team do last year," the other girl said. "You can't quit. We would be heartbroken if we didn't have a team."

This saddened me. I couldn't let these girls down.

"Would you girls be willing to recruit for the team?" I asked.

"YES! YES," they squealed.

"Okay, here's the plan," I said. "You go around campus and find two or three male students. They must have muscles and be big. If you find at least two and bring them down here this afternoon, we will keep this team going."

They literally ran out of my office.

Steve, my assistant, came to my office and asked how I was feeling. I told him about the two girls that had come in heartbroken because they thought we were going to cancel the rest of the acrobatic season.

He gave me a brief pep talk, as he always did, and ended by saying that we can do this.

About two hours later the two girls showed up with two big strapping guys I had never seen before, Ralph and Gilbert. They were from Miami and had never done any type of acrobatics.

Our experienced men (bases) began tutoring them. Right out of the gate, Ralph and Gilbert seemed to be having the time of their lives.

Within a week the whole team was charged up and the spirit was amazing.

"Heavy duty" was the new catch phrase, which Ralph and Gilbert said each time something went well.

Within a few weeks we had accomplished more than we had in the last year and a half. Everyone had really bought into what we were trying to accomplish and the spirit was fantastic.

We changed our name to Gym-Masters.

I learned a valuable lesson during those few weeks. It was the lesson of Gideon. I would rather have fewer teammates that were all pulling together than more talent but a team full of discontents.

I never forgot it for the rest of my coaching life.

By the end of the year we were so far ahead of what I believed was possible that I truly thought it was a miracle. After the Homeshow, our last show of the year, people were going crazy.

Even the president came up and congratulated me.

We had arrived!

That summer Steve and I went to a variety of clinics and shows, anything that had acrobatics included, to learn all we could.

By the end of the summer we were reinvigorated and ready to go. We just hoped we would have enough people with enough talent come to try out for next year's team.

RAISING THE BAR

In the third year, we had a new president. I didn't think at the time that this was significant, but I was so wrong—as you will see.

On the first night of tryouts we had about seventy-five students show up. I couldn't believe it. Our goal was to have thirty-two to thirty-eight on the team. However, the talent at tryouts was excellent and the excitement among the old team members was extraordinary.

After the two-week tryout period, Steve and I could not cut some deserving kids. We ended up with a team of forty.

For our third year, Steve and I were anxious to make the team not only a team that would recruit for Southern, but to somehow be a team that could be influential enough to make a difference in young people's lives.

We also wanted to raise the caliber of our team and our presentation so that we would be NBA-worthy. If we could accomplish both of those goals, then the recruiting aspect of our team would take care of itself. What kid would not like to perform at an NBA game in front of fifteen to twenty thousand people?

That year we were invited to do an assembly for a local high school. We decided to include some anti-drug skits in our program.

The team put the routines together and it went so much better than I could have ever imagined.

From that point on we began receiving requests from all over the local area for anti-drug assemblies. This was our "ah hah" moment, and we became known as America's Anti-Drug Acrobatic Team.

Our team goals changed to reflect our new mission:

1. Recruit for the college.

2. Promote the anti-drug life.

3. Create a once-in-a-lifetime experience for each student member.

That turned out to be a fabulous year. We had introduced a lot of new stunts and the team had really bought into our philosophy.

Homeshow again exceeded all expectations.

In year four we had almost two hundred people at tryouts. It was way beyond our wildest expectations, with students coming from all over the country.

Steve and I decided that we would make two cuts instead of one.

The talent was better than ever and the enthusiasm and spirit were outstanding. We kept the team at forty-two, and it was really tough to keep it at that number.

We had already decided that we were going to go to La Sierra in Southern California for their Acrobatic Clinic. We had never been there, but an acrobatic coach we knew told us that the La Sierra coach was constantly bragging about how they were the best acrobatic team in the SDA system.

Steve and I were both very competitive and so decided to accept the challenge and their invitation.

For the next six weeks we worked harder than we had ever worked before. Our goal was to have two first-rate routines ready for California.

On the last night of practice, we went through both routines twice, and they went like clockwork.

Following practice, Steve looked at me and said: "We're ready. Let's go kick butt."

Steve and I were so alike, we just couldn't stand to lose.

We flew out to California on Wednesday and took part in the clinic on Thursday and Friday.

Thursday night Steve and I were sitting in the dorm lobby reading the paper when a student walked in.

"Are you from Southern?" he asked. "I have heard you guys are really good."

"Thank you," I replied. "Are you on the La Sierra team?"

"Yes," he said.

"What kind of things do you do?" I asked.

"Well, to be honest, I'm not sure. I've only been to one practice," he responded.

Steve and I were both thinking the same thing. We knew how hard we had worked for the last six weeks to get ready. Hmmm?

Saturday night was the big show. We had been awarded two show slots and we couldn't wait to get started.

Our first routine went fabulously and the audience went crazy. I don't think they had ever seen anything quite like what we had just done.

Soon it was La Sierra's turn. The Master of Ceremonies (MC) introduced them with an excuse.

"La Sierra has not been in school for as long as some others," he said, "but they well do their best."

Their routine was, well, rough.

A short time later we were introduced for our second routine.

The MC pointed out to the audience that we had been in school longer than La Sierra.

Our second routine went great and again the audience went wild.

It was incredible.

After the show the kids and their parents swarmed us. It was as if we were celebrities.

Several coaches told me that we had surpassed Andrews as the number one acrobatic SDA college in America. They wondered how a couple of non-gymnastic jocks like Steve and I could have pulled this off.

I wanted to stay humble about it, which is not my best trait, but I knew we were indeed the best and going to get better.

When we got back home we sent a video to the Atlanta Hawks of the National Basketball Association, asking to do a halftime show for them.

EXCEEDING THE PRESIDENT'S EXPECTATIONS

*S*hortly after we returned from the west coast, the president sat down beside me at the cafeteria where I was waiting for Suzy.

"How's the gym team?" he asked.

"Great," I said.

"There are two things I expect you to accomplish with the team," he continued. "The first is that you need to build a program that is as good as the Andrews team. Second, your team needs to be a recruiting component for the university."

As quickly as he had joined me, he left, without giving me a chance to respond. Apparently, he had "something pressing" to attend to.

I didn't really know him as I had only met him a couple of times. I don't think he was at last year's Homeshow; at least I hadn't seen him.

This man exuded a pompous attitude like I had never seen. My first thoughts were—why don't you do your homework?

We are already considered the number one team of all SDA colleges. Every SDA high school in the country was imitating our moves and routines.

We had four new students try out for our team three years ago, and this year we had two hundred. We are doing more recruiting than has ever been done by the gymnastic team at Southern.

In our fifth year, we again had two hundred try out for the team. Each year the quality of the students improved, and it was becoming harder to turn them away.

In a conservative Christian school, acrobatic teams are going to get some criticisms. The typical audience at any SDA institution would run the gamut from ultra conservatives to very liberal.

The liberals don't say anything, but the ultra conservatives love to criticize—everything—our music, uniforms, and moves.

When the president received a letter from an ultra conservative, he would go ballistic.

For the next seven years, he harassed me continuously.

After one trip, he pointed out how upsetting it was that he had received two letters criticizing our performance.

He insisted that I be *very* careful, as good PR was important.

I asked him what he personally thought about the aspects of our performance that were mentioned in the complaint.

He couldn't tell me—because he hadn't seen us perform.

Unbelievable!

He did take the time, however, to tell to me that he might come out and play some floor hockey in the intramural program. He boasted about being from Canada and that he was a great ice hockey player.

I played in the intramural floor hockey league and at times there was some heavy duty hitting. I sure wish he *had* brought his talents out and played.

On Monday, after the Homeshow that year, we received a phone call from the Atlanta Hawks.

The NBA playoffs were starting Thursday night and their halftime performers had cancelled. Would we be willing to take their place?

Are you kidding!

Absolutely! This was our big opportunity.

The entertainment coordinator gave me the rundown on how everything would work.

When our team was announced, we would have seven minutes to get our mats on the floor, set up, do our routine, get the mats up, and be off the floor. If we were one second late, we would never be invited back.

"Yes ma'am, that will not be a problem," I said.

On Tuesday and Wednesday we practiced hard, including bringing the mats in, setting up, doing the routine, and then getting our mats off the floor.

Our routine by itself ran for five minutes, not counting the setup and take down. Steve and I debated about whether we should shorten it.

We decided we could do it.

Thursday night came and we were at the Omni in Atlanta, Georgia.

This is what we had wanted for several years. This was our chance. Our music man was taken to their sound booth and they would start the music on my signal.

The game had started and halftime was approaching.

I don't know about anyone else, but I was pumped.

As the first half was nearing its end, the coordinator told me to get everyone in place.

"Don't go out until the announcer is completely finished with his introduction," she said. "I will be right here to say go."

There it is!

"Ladies and gentleman, for your halftime enjoyment we present, from Southern College, America's Anti-Drug Acrobatic Team."

"GO!" she said, and we were off.

We carried our mats in and set them up, including putting down the straps to hold the seven sections together.

We hustled to our spots and wouldn't you know, one of our guys was completely lost. Someone finally told him where to go and as soon as he got into position, I gave the signal for the music and we were off and running.

The routine went beautifully, we did the ending pose, and then I yelled GO!

We tore the mats down rolled them up and headed out the door.

The crowd was going crazy and gave us a standing ovation.

When we were out of the stadium, we were laughing and cheering. The coordinator told us how wonderful we were.

The whole process, including the entry, the setup, the routine, the tear down, and getting off the floor, was completed in six minutes and forty seconds.

Everybody cheered.

Later, the coordinator talked to me.

"Ted, I have gotten your videos these past years, but you know, videos never do justice to any act," she said. "You guys were fantastic. Halftime performances never get a standing ovation. You guys brought down the house."

She went on to tell me that she virtually never takes acts from church or school groups because, while mom's and dad's think their kids are great, their performances are never good enough for this event.

"Are you interested in allowing one of our girls to sing the National Anthem?" I asked.

"Ted, you know what kind of quality we are looking for," she said. "Does she qualify?"

"Absolutely!" I answered.

"I don't doubt you," she said. "Next time you're here we will put her on the schedule. What is her name?"

"Holly Jones," I said.

That summer we got calls and invitations from NBA teams from all over the country.

The Hawks coordinator had passed the word on about us.

Over the next five years we did halftime shows for NBA teams in Charlotte, Orlando, Miami, Indianapolis, Washington DC, Chicago, Detroit, Cleveland, Philadelphia, New York, New Jersey, Boston, Golden State, and Sacramento.

We performed at more SDA schools and public schools than ever before with the funds provided by the NBA.

As an interesting note, we, the Southern College Anti-Drug Team, became the number two ranked NBA halftime show behind the Bud Light Daredevils.

The next time we went to Atlanta, Holly was also scheduled to sing the National Anthem.

We arrived early and Holly, the coordinator, and I went through the logistics of how Holly would get into position, sing, and then leave.

We all agreed that when Holly was finished, she would walk straight out to where I would be standing waiting for her.

As the time approached, Holly and I got into position and then, on cue, she continued to center court.

The lights went off and the spotlights were focused on Holly.

She sang beautifully and the crowd loved it.

As she was coming off the floor, she was looking directly at me, or so I thought, but then suddenly she turned right and walked right in front of the Hawks team.

One of the largest guys on the team, Kevin Willis, said in his deep voice, "Awesome baby!" as she walked by.

When I finally caught up with her, she said she had no idea where she was going and had not seen me, or heard the player congratulate her.

The coordinator loved Holly, and our entire team was super proud of her.

While the NBA performances were fun and exciting, they were never our main focus.

This is what some of our critics didn't understand, including the president.

What the NBA did for us was to provide the funds by which we could travel.

A lot of SDA acrobatic teams went to places like Puerto Rico to help build schools or churches, however Steve and I decided that there is a real need right here at home.

The recruiting for Southern and the anti-drug program at the public schools remained our main mission.

GOD WAS WATCHING OVER US

In our sixth year, the team received a sponsorship from Trans World Airlines.

During spring break, we took advantage of the TWA sponsorship and flew to the west coast where we were booked to do several SDA school programs and anti-drug assemblies, and one NBA halftime.

After the flight to San Francisco, we had arranged with a SDA academy to make available a bus and driver to escort us around Northern California.

We arrived at the airport around 12:00 noon, but there was no sign of the bus that was supposed to pick us up.

The driver had driven for us before and I knew he was responsible. I expected he would arrive shortly.

After an hour or so, I called the high school he worked for. He had left at around 9:00 a.m. for the two-hour drive and he should have been here by now.

At 4:00 p.m. I called the school again, but they had not heard from him. I told them we needed to be at the Golden State Warriors arena by six, so we were going to rent vans.

I started the rental process and had all the keys in my hand when one of the team members ran up and said the driver had arrived.

I cancelled the vans and we loaded up and headed for Oakland.

"Hello, how are you?" I said when we were on the bus.

"Fine," he responded.

"Did you have trouble?" I asked.

"No trouble," he said.

Okay, so what's going on, I wondered.

Forty-five minutes later, we arrived at the Warriors' arena. The team unloaded the bus and then we parked in the designated area.

Steve took the team into the arena and I stayed to talk to the driver.

"We are doing the halftime show and then loading up to go to Pacific Union College, our sister college in the Napa Valley," I explained. "We're not staying for the second half of the game, so you need to meet us at 9:00 back at the loading area where we just unloaded."

"Okay," he said.

I hustled in and met the halftime coordinator to get my instructions.

Halftime came and our performance went well. We loaded up our mats and equipment and headed out to the loading area. One problem; the bus wasn't there.

We checked the area where I had last seen the bus, and it was still there, minus the driver.

Steve and I organized a search party, searching the parking area, and even in the basement of the arena.

No driver.

We decided to wait for the game to finish and then make a decision. We still had a two-hour-plus drive and we needed to eat.

At around 10:30 the fans started pouring out of the arena. We stood around and waited. At around 11:15 the driver walked up, opened up the bus, got in, and started the motor.

We drove to the loading area, picked up our mats and equipment, and headed out at around 11:45.

I was beside myself; what is going on?

As we drive I am looking for a fast food place to get something to eat, but everything looked closed.

Finally, I see a Taco Bell that appeared to be open.

We pull in and they were only open for drive-through. I walked up to the drive-through window and asked if I could order eighty bean burritos for the group on the bus.

"Are you kidding?" they said. "No!"

We didn't eat that night.

On several occasions during the rest of the trip, the driver went perilously close to the side of the road, sometimes swerving suddenly for no apparent reason.

None of us got any sleep, as we were all concerned about the driver and the way he was driving.

The last seven miles to PUC are up a steep hill that has many twist and turns, so I stood next to the driver; just in case intervention was needed.

We arrived at PUC around 2:30 a.m., put our mats out in the gym, and finally were able to get to sleep at around 3:00.

The next morning an aerobics class met in the gym at 6:00. They started blasting their music without a thought for the tired group of Gym-Masters.

At 11:00 a.m., we did an assembly program for the PUC students.

After they fed us, we loaded the bus and headed for Lodi, California.

During the trip, I sat by the driver and carried on a conversation. When we arrived at the host high school in Lodi, we were all relieved.

We were extremely tired, but more importantly, we were all thankful that God had been watching over us.

At Lodi, I talked to my former roommate, Jerry, and told him about our experience with the driver. Jerry was a member of the board at Lodi Academy, the school the driver worked for.

"The driver is supposed to take a group of students snow skiing in a couple of days," Jerry said. "My daughters are scheduled to go. Would you let him drive?"

"Jerry, there's something wrong here," I said, "and there is no way I would let him drive."

After our spring break trip, Jerry called me with some sobering news. The driver had been diagnosed with an inoperable brain tumor. He passed away a few weeks later.

We felt sorry for the driver, and again, thanked God for his protection.

THERE'S NO PLACE FOR "MEAN"

O ver the next five years, the president continued to receive letters from the ultra conservatives, and I continued to be called into his office.

One especially harrowing incident was when the representative from Mississippi came into my office and asked if we could come to his school the following weekend.

We were not scheduled to perform at that particular school that year, but they asked us to attend anyway. We had to decline as we were already booked, to do an anti-drug assembly, and an NBA half-time that same weekend.

He complained to the president about what he considered an inappropriate photo in my office of our team at a water park in their swimsuits, and the fact that we were putting an NBA team ahead of them.

The president called me in and berated me about the photo, and yet he had never seen it. He found it reprehensible that I would put an NBA show ahead of the SDA school, and to "get that photo off your wall."

I would have liked to explain to him that we schedule each SDA school every other year, just as we had always done according to school policy.

I would also have liked to have told him about how the representative from the Mississippi school had come to us at the last minute on a year they were not scheduled, but as usual, I was not given the opportunity.

On another occasion, the president called me in and told me the Mississippi representative and his son had been at an NBA game at which we performed. They were appalled that we appeared to be ashamed of our name as we were announced as Southern College, instead of Southern College of Seventh-day Adventists.

"Why do you even perform for the NBA?" he asked. It was so bizarre that he asked this same question almost every time he was chastising me, but would never let me give our rationale.

I would have liked to have explained to him what our goals were and how the NBA helped finance those opportunities, but he didn't give me a chance to respond. Neither he, nor the Mississippi representative, ever found out why the introduction was announced like it was. There was a logical explanation, but I was never given the opportunity to explain that the NBA halftime coordinators tried to keep church affiliations out of the spotlight as it could create further conflicts with other denominations who could want equal time.

The president was our biggest critic, and even if I had been allowed to explain, he would never buy into my rationale.

The better we became, the more in demand we were. Our yearly schedule had always included one-half of the SDA high schools in the southeastern United States, and they always had precedence in the scheduling process.

We encouraged these schools to schedule us when they had special weekends of spiritual emphasis, as we liked to be a part of these weekends.

Highland Academy was a SDA high school a few miles north of Nashville. As was our scheduling protocol, two years in advance of their special spiritual weekend they invited us to come and be involved. We would close the weekend with our acrobatic program.

Late scheduling by Southern meant that weekend was also their week of prayer. Students and the various groups were discouraged from scheduling off-campus appointments for that weekend. Dorm students were allowed to leave, but were encouraged to stay.

As we had made this appointment two years in advance, we felt obligated to go.

We left for Highland Academy on Friday morning. That evening we were included in their spiritual activities. Later that night, our team sat around and talked about how great this experience had already been for them. They felt they had really bonded with the Highland kids.

I knew then that it was going to be a fulfilling weekend.

Saturday was filled with a variety of spiritual activities and our team really invested themselves. Saturday night our team performed our road show, which ended with a spiritual emphasis.

Several of the faculty, and the principal, told our team how wonderful the weekend had been. The faculty felt that their kids had gained so much because of our interaction with them.

Our team had really been touched by this weekend, and probably got just as much or more from their kids.

On our trip home, the team told stories of the kids they had been involved with and they loved the spiritual blessing they had received through their interactions over the weekend.

Arriving home, that wonderful spirit took a terrible turn for the worse.

Our team learned that the president was chastizing us and was disgusted that we had left campus and gone to Highland during the college's week of prayer.

The team was devastated.

The president did not talk to me directly and would not take my calls. When I tried to get an appointment, I was told he had no openings.

That week he addressed the Faculty Senate and told them how disgraceful it was that we had left the college at the end of the week of prayer.

Shortly after the meeting, a faculty member told me about his tirade.

I thought: Oh boy, here we go again. He goes off when he knows only half of the story.

I asked the faculty member if he could get me on the agenda for next week's Faculty Senate.

"Absolutely, I'm sure everyone would like to hear from you."

The next week I addressed the Faculty Senate.

I told them how cramped our schedule was and that we were scheduling two years in advance. The on-campus spiritual weekend here at Southern was planned just this past summer, while the Highland trip had been scheduled a year and a half earlier.

I told them about the wonderful spiritual experience it had been for us, and yet when we returned home, how hurtful it was that the president was condemning us.

I was hoping the president would have been at the Faculty Senate meeting to hear my presentation, but he wasn't there.

It was consistent with his M.O. as he didn't want to hear my explanation as to why this had happened.

Two members of the Faculty Senate talked to me during the week and gave me their perspective.

"The president is a power hungry little man and he hates the accolades you and the Gym-Masters have received," one said. "We believe he will try to bring you and the team down, and would be happy if the team didn't exist at all."

After my faculty presentation, I remember thinking that it sure was a lot easier when we were no good and nobody cared about us.

And just when I thought it couldn't get any worse, a curious thing happened.

We had brought in a magician to be a time-filler between our routines at Homeshow.

Before we had officially hired him, we discussed several of my concerns.

I told him all about our school and the conservative beliefs of SDA.

He said his show was totally G-rated and suggested that he would send me a tape of one of his performances.

After I watched the tape, I was confident there would be no problem.

During the show he did several skits and magic acts, and they were exactly what I had hoped for: appropriate and entertaining.

Then in one of his last skits, he lit up a cigarette as part of his act.

Oh no! I'm going to hear about this, I thought.

A few days later the president called me in and pretty much went berserk about the magician and the cigarette routine.

"You don't have enough sense to check out a thing like this before you hire somebody?" he asked.

I explained how thoroughly I had checked him out.

"Well it sure wouldn't have happened if I had been in charge," he responded.

END OF AN ERA

During my tenth year, we were invited to do a halftime performance for the Atlanta Falcons on Monday Night Football.

The student newspaper did an article about the performance, and included a team photo, for the front page.

I heard that this had made the president furious.

That week the president called me in, upset about the whole NFL performance.

"Why would you take our students out of school for this?" he raged. "I don't see any benefit to Southern at all."

That spring we were featured in the national magazine, "LISTEN". They praised us for our influence in helping to fight the drug problem facing young people all over America.

I remember thinking that maybe now the president would see what our mission and contribution truly was, but I heard nothing.

A few months later, during the summer, the president called me in. His Administrative Assistant (AA) was also in the room, and he had something to say.

"You think you and your team are professional quality, but you're not. Just because you perform for the NBA doesn't mean you're professional quality. The Russian pair you brought in for your clinic, they're professional quality. You're not even close."

I sat there in disbelief.

The president then took over. "This is not going to be a discussion, but a statement," he said. "I am not going to permit you to continue running the program the way it has been run. In the future, you will not be allowed to go to NBA or NFL games.

"Furthermore, I must not get complaints about your music, moves, uniforms, etc. In the future you will change the program so that these complaints never happen again."

Even though I knew how he was, and was warned that he was out to get me, I felt totally blindsided.

Ten years ago, I began a journey to make the acrobatic team something special. This was no small task, especially for a person with no background in the sport.

Now we were the consensus number one ranked SDA acrobatic team and trendsetters—every SDA high school and college were trying to emulate our tricks and routines.

I just couldn't believe this was happening, and felt totally hurt and unappreciated.

I stared at the president. How could a person with his lack of Christian character be allowed to be president of any SDA institution?

I stood up and said: "If that's what you want, you've got the wrong guy in the head coach position."

"If you quit the team you don't have a job at Southern," he responded.

I walked to the front of his desk and said: "You do what you have to do and I'll do what I have to do." And walked out.

I was sick about this whole situation. I was mad at the president, his sidekick, the SDA people in Mississippi and their representative, who all seemed to think they were the moral conscience of the Gym-Masters program.

I asked the Lord: Why? What do you have in store for me?

I sometimes wondered why I had ever gotten involved with the SDA church and school system.

Most of my best friends are SDAs and I love and respect them, but there are so many legalistic hypocrites in SDA leadership positions that have little or no Christian attributes.

I almost hoped he would indeed fire me and let me be rid of this occupational abuse.

After I left the president's office, I had no idea what I was going to do. I already had some coaching offers in the public-school system. Maybe this was the right time to make the move.

On the other hand, I had worked so hard on creating an acrobatic team and anti-drug program that was deemed so effective, I hated to walk away from it.

The president, I soon learned, had insulted and burned his bridges with many others. Several encouraged me to keep the faith and don't let him be my stumbling block (Matthew 18:7-9).

This man, it appears, has been a stumbling block to many.

Fortunately for me, Steve volunteered to take over the Gym-Masters team, and I stayed at Southern for another six or seven years.

Unfortunately, the longer I stayed, the more disenchanted I became with the SDA church, its practices, judgmental attitudes, and traditional legalistic stances.

It was time for me to find Jesus Christ and a mission field without an anchor of SDA church doctrines hung around my neck.

I knew I had some talent and could coach, lead, and help inspire young people. I had, after all, taken over the leadership of two programs, the men's fastpitch team and the Gym-Masters, and had lead both programs from last to first.

I was confident I would do it again.

COACHING AGAIN

❦

The ladies softball teams at Chattanooga State, Armstrong State, and Bryan College became my mission field.

Over the next sixteen years I discovered that some of these ladies were devoted Christians, and it showed in the way they lived their lives. They were kind, accepting, helpful, and full of love for all.

Many others had struggles with being a Christian. They had grown up in a strict religious home and they had rebelled.

They were from a number of different denominations, and most of them eventually stopped going to church. They had made Christian commitments and then given them up for one reason or another.

Home became a battleground for them, and some parents all but disowned them.

Some expressed a desire to be a Christian again and were anxious to find the right recipe for a long and consistent Christian life. This sentiment became the inspiration for writing this book.

I had just accepted the position of assistant softball coach at Chattanooga State. This would be my mission field, just as dad had impressed on Tim and me when we went to public elementary school.

I wanted to make this adventure my new Christian focus.

However, I found it hard to be a good Christian and, at the same time, hold a grudge against the SDA church and its leaders. There seemed to be a tug of war in my heart as the SDA doctrines were so ingrained in my soul.

As time went on, I realized that there are good and strong Christians in every faith and I was slowly able to put aside most of my SDA contempt and focus almost solely on Christ and becoming more like him.

Three years later I accepted the head softball coach position at Armstrong State in Savannah, Georgia.

Helping this team to become a championship-quality team wasn't going to be easy. The team from the previous year had done well, but twelve girls didn't return when their coach left.

We had one starter left on the roster, and a total of eleven girls. In the second semester I was able to pick up two additional girls; this gave us thirteen. Most teams carry eighteen to twenty-four players.

That first year was rough and I was hoping that we could at least be respectable. Like any first-year coach, I had to deal with the "That's not how we used to do it" attitudes.

By the end of the year we stood at twenty-one wins and twenty-one losses. This was incredible considering the limited talent and the pessimistic attitudes.

I couldn't wait to remove those that didn't want to be there, or were not buying into my program.

I knew that, as with the Gym-Masters, I may lose some talent, but we would be much better off when we were all pulling together as a team.

That summer I recruited hard and landed some great new talent.

I was quite rigid about my views on being a team and a family. I had learned that it is much more important that girls' teams get along than it is for guys' teams.

If the girls were not getting along together, it really affected the play on the field.

We did a variety of things from the very beginning of school to encourage team unity. We had scavenger hunts, parties at my house, Christmas gift exchanges, and many other team-bonding activities.

We conducted my favorite team activity just before the official season started, and named it, "the rose ceremony."

In the middle of the floor was a vase with two dozen roses. Each girl was given a team list and they would write a positive thought about each of their fellow teammates.

The girls kept secret what they had written.

At the rose ceremony, a blank piece of paper was taped on everyone's back. Then the girls would transfer their thoughts to the backs of their teammates.

When this exercise was completed, we talked about how we all had good and bad traits. The rose signified this with its conflicting traits: a beautiful flower and thorns.

We can all see the beauty in our teammates. If we focus on the positive, we will play better and have a much better chance of reaching our goals.

I then challenged them to only think positive thoughts. To accept the challenge, they needed to take a rose to signify their commitment.

That year attitudes improved, and we were a much better team as a result. We ended the year with forty wins and twenty losses, and made the NCAA Regional Tournament.

We were off and running.

I stayed at the university for twelve years.

There are approximately two hundred and fifty schools in NCAA Division 2. Every school would dearly love to make it to the Division 2 World Series, which hosts only the eight best teams in the nation.

To get there you must be ranked as one of the top sixty-four teams in America, and then you must win two tournaments against the other sixty-three teams.

This is a very difficult task and most coaches never experience the thrill of getting to the World Series.

We got there *three times*.

The first time was during my ninth year, and we finishing third.

In my tenth year, we were once again regional champions and played in the World Series.

We were beat out in my eleventh year and the team that went through from our region, won the national tournament. They had an outstanding pitcher and she won the National Pitcher of the Year Award.

In my twelfth and last year, we had to play the reigning champs—who still had their outstanding pitcher.

It was a best out of three, and they beat us convincingly in the first game, their pitcher allowing only one hit.

The next day we had to win two games. We won the first game—the overall score, one-all.

In the third and final game, our team jumped out to a 3 to 0 advantage. In the bottom of the seventh inning, all we needed was three outs and, for the third time in four years, we would be going back to the World Series.

But our opponents didn't flinch and got two on with two out. The batter was their left fielder who was an outstanding player, but not a threat to hit a home run; in fact she was a senior and had never hit a home run in college.

The count went to three balls and two strikes. The next pitch came in down the middle and a little high, and the batter hit the first home run of her career.

The score was tied.

I couldn't believe it. We now had to go to extra innings.

In the top of the eighth, one of our girls hit a two-run homer—and we had defeated the reigning national champions and the pitcher of the year.

We returned to the D2 World Series and finished fourth.

After my third World Series, a colleague approached me and said: "Ted, you should be so proud. I have been trying to get to the World Series for thirty years. You have been there three out of the last four years, that's incredible. I just hope I can get there once before I stop coaching."

After I had time to stop and digest it all, I felt a sense of satisfaction; we had accomplished so much. It would have been great to win a national championship, but only one team can do that out of two hundred and fifty each year.

We came close three times. That is something to be very proud of.

WHY, LORD? WHY?

About three years after leaving the Gym-Masters program at Southern, my dad fell ill, and then contracted pneumonia.

Clyde and Tim were both in California with dad, and Clyde told me that he thought dad would pull through.

I asked to talk to dad and Clyde gave him the phone. He sounded very frail.

"I'm coming to see you, Dad," I said.

"That's good, hurry," he said weakly.

Finally, I said: "Dad, I love you."

"I love you, too," he said.

Those were the last words I ever heard him say. Before I could get home, my hero was gone. I was heartbroken.

One evening after dad's funeral, mom and I went for a walk.

We talked about our past and we both conceded that we should have handled things much better. We both wanted there to be a second chance and it should start now.

From that time on, things were so much better and more positive between us.

During the NCAA regional play in my fourth year at Armstrong, I received a phone call from Tim. He said mom had called him and said that Clyde had had an accident of some sort. They had found him unconscious in a public bathroom.

"The hospital won't talk to me and want you to call them," he said.

I called the hospital and they gave me the devastating news.

Clyde had a brain aneurysm that had burst. He was being kept alive, but was in a coma.

"What are his chances of surviving this?" I asked.

"I'm sorry to tell you this, but we are keeping him alive so that we can harvest his organs," the hospital representative said. "We need your permission to keep him alive until that process can begin."

I knew this is what Clyde would have wanted. This would be his last gift to those with needs. I called Tim and told him the news.

"They want our permission to let them harvest his organs," I said. "Are you okay with that?"

"Absolutely," Tim replied.

I gave the okay to proceed.

How could this be? Clyde was only sixty-three and he was the most clean-living person I had ever known.

Tim said he would go to New York and take care of things. During the next few days we received dozens of cards and letters expressing condolences.

The stories about Clyde were always the same.

He was always there for everyone and always wanting to help. He was such a giver, one of his friends wrote. That definitely brought back memories.

A short while later we received a report from the medical group that had harvested his organs. They began by saying that Clyde's organs were like those of a thirty-year-old.

A few weeks later we were given a medallion from the Gift of Life Society, awarding Clyde the Medal of Honor for his donations. I still have and cherish that medallion.

About three years later, Tim had a mental breakdown and he and his wife split up. I spent several weeks with him, trying to help him through a tough time.

A short time later, mom moved to Lodi so that she could live close to Tim. She wasn't doing real well herself, and had lost her driving privileges.

One day I got a call from Tim's ex-wife stating that mom had fallen on her way to the bank.

She had fallen while stepping over the curb and couldn't get up. Thankfully, she wasn't hurt too badly.

Suzy and I went out to California to make an assessment. When we saw mom, she had become weaker physically and her mental capabilities had certainly eroded.

We decided to take her back to Georgia with us.

This turned out to be a special time for me and mom. For most of my life, our relationship had been difficult, and now here we were, living together.

I remember thinking that it was ironic that I was the son who would be taking care of her, the son who had given her such a hard time growing up. Maybe this was the Lord's way of putting us back together for both of our sakes.

Either way, I was grateful for the opportunity to be reacquainted with her.

As mom continued to decline, it became more and more difficult to have her live in our home.

We had a sitter stay with her when we were at work, but mom was not happy with this arrangement and would often leave the house if the sitter turned her back.

We finally put her in a retirement home close to where Suzy and I worked. She seemed much more content there. It helped that they had a piano, and she played it daily.

One morning I got a call from the retirement home. Mom had fallen and had broken her hip and arm. She had also hit her head.

When we got to the home, the doctor had been there and left his telephone number for me to call.

"She is going to have a tough time getting through this," he said. "If she survives for seventy-two hours, she might recover."

I spent most of the day with her. She didn't want to eat and her awareness of her surroundings was fluctuating.

I sat there looking at the woman that was my mom. We had so many conflicts as I grew up. Over the last couple of years, it was amazing how well we had gotten along. I know it was a great blessing for me and I hoped it was for her as well.

Suzy came by after work and brought us some food. Mom was getting progressively weaker and more disconsolate.

Finally, before we left for the night, I said: "Mom, Suzy and I are going to leave now; we will see you in the morning."

She opened her eyes and looked at me.

"I love you, Mom," I said.

She gave me a diminutive smile and said weakly, "I love you, too, Ted".

Those were the last words I ever heard her say and they will be ingrained in my heart forever.

I praise the Lord that I had these last two years, and especially this last moment, with my mom.

Six months later we received a phone call from the retirement home that Tim had moved into. They had found Tim, in his bed, not breathing. He'd had a heart attack and was gone.

This was especially difficult for me. Tim and I had always been so close, especially growing up, but even as adults we stayed close.

We talked sports a lot. During football season, we talked every week and played a little game with the point spreads of the NFL games. It was always fun and gave us an enjoyable way of staying close.

To add to the difficulty of his death, Tim was the last of my immediate family to pass. It was a strange feeling to be the only one left.

Tim's son made the decision to have him buried in a military cemetery. Dad, mom, and Clyde were all buried at their church cemetery. I wished Tim could have been buried with them, but I felt I needed to let his son and daughter make the final decision.

The military burial service was wonderful, but as with all funerals, it was so final.

I still miss my best buddy!

GOD MUST BE LEADING

*N*ow that I had retired, Suzy and I had a decision to make. Where do we go to live out our retirement? What kind of home do we want to live in? We had never lived in a condominium, but we thought that might be a possibility.

We had friends and some of my family in Northern California, and friends and some of Suzy's family in Chattanooga, Tennessee.

After doing some research, we discovered that prices in California were so much higher than Tennessee that it made sense to look there first.

My good friend Steve looked around for us and said there was a really nice condo village that he would check out for us. He called back later that day and said the condos are all one story and there was one for sale that had our friend Ron's name on the realtor listing sign.

I called Ron and asked him about the property. He said it had just come on the market. Suzy was pretty excited about the condo idea. She thought it might be the perfect lifestyle change for us as we went into retirement. She convinced me when she said, "You would have no yard work and could play more golf." YAHOO!

"How soon could you come and see it," he asked.

"Anytime," I replied.

"The properties at this complex are very popular and don't last long," he said. "Could you come tomorrow?"

"Yes," I said, "we will see you at eleven."

If this had been anybody other than an old friend, that I fully trusted, it would have sounded like one of those "better be quick" sales pitches.

Suzy was hoping this one would work out. We looked up photos online and didn't think it looked all that impressive.

We met Ron at the property, which looked a lot better on the outside than the online photos suggested. The small community in which it was located looked really quiet and classy.

We went inside.

The entryway was nice and the sunroom off to the left was impressive. Then there was a living/dining great room with the kitchen off to the side of the dining room.

It was beautiful!

I stopped and turned around. Suzy stood there almost as if she was in a trance, with a tear in her eye.

I walked back and asked: "Are you all right?"

"This is it," she said.

We paused for an instant and then went on to see the bedrooms, bathrooms, laundry room, and garage.

I really liked it, too.

We made an offer that day and it was accepted.

How could it be that things had worked out so nicely for us?

"This is our last home," Suzy said. "I never want to move again."

We could just feel it; we were indeed, home.

A short time later, I went to my old driving range where I had taught golf classes for eighteen years.

There was another fellow there hitting, and we were not too far apart. Next thing you know, we were talking about golf and then we introduced ourselves.

His name was Jerry Arnold, and I told him my name was Ted Evans.

"Ted Evans. I've heard about you," he said.

He was the pastor of the Collegedale Community Church (CCC). I thought he was probably lying because he was not a good enough golfer to be an SDA minister. However, I really enjoyed playing golf with him because, as you know, I really hate to lose.

I told him that my wife and I were not currently attending any church. He got excited and began telling me all about the CCC church; how different it was and how I needed to come and see it for myself.

Was this providence, or just a chance meeting, I thought.

Having now been to the church, it is different. Pastor Arnold really stimulates spiritual thinking and we feel we have received a blessing each time we have attended.

There were several other incidents that were all adding up to what seemed like extraordinary coincidences. One might conclude that God had his hand in leading Suzy and me back to the Collegedale area.

The last by-chance meeting was with a former student, Ernest Dempsey.

I ran into Ernie at the Collegedale Academy golf tournament. There were around one hundred and fifty participants and organizers there and yet somehow, I bumped into and got into a discussion with Ernie.

He told me how much he had enjoyed my golf class some twenty years ago, and as we talked, I asked him what line of work he was in. He said he wrote books.

Unbelievable, I thought.

I explained to Ernie that I had just finished this, my first book, and didn't have a clue how to get it published.

As a very successful writer, he knew all of the nuances of the book publishing process and he quickly volunteered to be my mentor.

"This is an amazing coincidence," I said.

"This is not a coincidence," Ernie replied.

I knew he was right.

This book is a testimony to the fact that Ernie has done exactly what he said he would do.

Soon after we moved back to the Chattanooga area, I got word that a small Christian College was looking for a hitting coach for their women's fastpitch team.

I thought it sounded intriguing so I talked to the new coach.

She had been a very successful high school coach, but this was her first experience in college. She and I talked for a couple of hours and I liked her from the start. She was confident, but not so proud that she couldn't glean ideas from and old geezer like me.

The coach wanted to hear more about me and my hitting system. We spent most of our time together talking about it. She then told me she had some other interviews and would get back in touch with me in a few days.

When she called back, she offered me the position of assistant coach.

"I have one question," I said. "Will I be the hitting coach?"

"Yes," she said.

"I was never a pitching coach, so I hired one and stayed out of it," I said. I wanted to clarify my position. "Here is what I say to you. My hitting system has steps to success. No one else can interject their thoughts and instruction into it. It just doesn't work that way."

"I understand," she said. "It's all yours."

From that point on we went to work.

The year went better than most people expected. Our team was picked, preseason, to finish fifth or sixth in the conference; we beat the odds and tied for first.

During the year, two or three ladies on the team gave testimonials. They were heart-warming and heart-wrenching at the same time.

One particular girl talked about how she had stopped going to church and became involved with a pretty wild crowd, and that her parents all but disowned her. When she decided to once again be a Christian, she wasn't ready to go back to her old church. Nobody was happy with her decision. Her friends wanted nothing to do with her and her parents were even more frustrated with her than before.

At one of the worship sessions, I gave my testimony to the softball ladies. It was an emotional time for them, and for me. These ladies had been a real blessing and inspiration to me. I expressed to them how hard it could be to find a consistent Christian life. I hoped that no matter where they were in their Christian experience they would each find peace through a relationship with Jesus Christ.

In my life, I explained, there were plenty of hot and cold times in my Christian experience. I had often seen church signs that read, "The Lord is coming, ARE YOU READY?"

I had over the years tried so hard to "get ready." Each time I eventually failed. I just could not be "good" enough, so I gave up.

Clyde once told me a story about a man that slipped and fell into some deep water. The man could not swim and was thrashing around trying to save himself, but he couldn't. A young man, who was a good swimmer, waited for the drowning man to run out of energy and give up. The young man then jumped in and saved the drowning man.

This is a lot like me. I had on so many occasions felt defeated. I was trying too hard to save myself but I couldn't, when all I had to do was to reach out and ask, "Lord, save me".

I discovered that I could never be good enough. I was proud and thought I could succeed in being a Christian by my own efforts. I had missed the most important message. God is waiting with outstretched arms, and being a Christian is his gift. All I needed to do was ask him to come into my life and be my savior (John 3:15-17; John 6:40; John 11:25.26; Revelation 3:20).

I have asked myself numerous times why it is so difficult for some, like me, to have a consistent Christian life, and so easy for others, like my brother Clyde. I believe that, at least for me, "pride" was at the core of my failures in my pursuit to attain a consistent Christian life.

Jesus is knocking at your door. Humble yourself and ask him to come into your life and be your savior, and eternal life is yours.

THE FOLLOWING IS a list that Suzy and I have found to be critically important components for us to maintain a consistent Christian life.

1. **Ask God to come into your heart every day.** Ask God to let his

Spirit permeate your soul and help you be a kinder, gentler person and emulate Jesus.

2. **Trust God.** There will always be things we do not understand about the way God works. This is when we must have faith in what we don't understand. As you look back on your life, be thankful for God's leading.

3. **Associate with good people.** Church can be a great place to find strength and support. It helps immensely when your best friend(s) or mate is right there to give encouragement and support.

4. **Spend time with Jesus each day.** Ask him for strength. Study his word and let the Holy Spirit speak to you, guide you, and help you grow in your relationship with him.

5. **Be a giver. Find ways to help others.** This does not necessarily have to be monumental tasks. Opening a door for the elderly or remembering others birthdays lets people know you care. Many are hurting; just listening can be very therapeutic.

6. **Share God's love.** Be willing to let people know how wonderful your God is and how much you appreciate his effect on your life. Let God's love be seen in you.

7. **See the good in all people.** We are all like roses: with thorns, but also a beautiful flower. I ask God every day to help me put aside my intolerance and see the positives in everyone.

GOD'S WAITING, ARMS OUTSTRETCHED!

*I*t seems to be the general consensus of most Christians that the longer one nurtures a relationship with Jesus Christ, the stronger and more enduring the relationship becomes. In so doing, Christ becomes our friend, and sustaining a consistent Christian life becomes more natural and effortless.

This is not to say that there won't be challenges and difficulties in the Christian walk. This is a sinful and imperfect world, but with Jesus Christ as our friend and ally we will be bolstered, comforted, and rejuvenated.

I asked a number of friends, who I consider to be devout Christians, their thoughts on how to gain and maintain a consistent Christian life. These Christians are from a variety of denominations. Following are their responses.

It is my hope that you will find strength and commitment in the thoughts of these Christians and find your own walk with God.

GUIDANCE FROM TANYA:

Q: What do you do on a regular basis to maintain a consistent Christian life?

I start the day with prayer and like to keep praying throughout the day, talking to God out loud, or in my thoughts, and I don't say, "Amen". I want to keep our conversation going. I can talk to Him about anything and I know He's listening to me. Sometimes I'll write out my prayers like a letter to a friend. When I pray, I feel God's presence and know He influences my thoughts and actions by filling me with His spirit. I consider my prayer with God an honest conversation with a friend. I think He likes that, too.

I also like taking time each morning to read my Bible and a devotional thought. Before opening the pages, I think it's important to pray for the Holy Spirit's leading and influence, for God to teach me in His Word. There are two powers at work in this universe, and I want only the Power of God to influence my mind; that goes for everything I do throughout the day. There's Light and there's Darkness, and I always want to choose the Light. I invite God to use me every day and pray that the Holy Spirit will help me grow and become closer to God. There's a song I sing every morning. The words are from a little book called Steps to Jesus. "Take me O Lord, I'm wholly yours, I lay all my plans at your feet. Use me today in your service. Live with me and let all I do be done to honor You." It's a good way to start each day.

Singing has always been a big part of my life. As a child, I sang with my family at little country churches and gatherings in the mountains of East Tennessee. We had so much fun. I still love to sing and have realized that if I put Scripture to song I can memorize it so much easier. Music is such a gift of God. The birds sing praises all day long, never tiring as they sing to the creator. I'm thankful for the example they are; such gentle, joyful creatures.

I believe church is a very important place where we can be spiritually fed and grow in our Christian walk. I have been blessed with wonderful pastors who reflect a loving, caring God. Church has provided me with a community of believers who can talk and pray together, supporting each other, a family. God calls us to come apart from the busy world and take a day to rest in Him, living for Him. It's definitely not something I can do on my own, only with His help and goodness, joy, patience, and forgiveness. He says to us, "If you love me, keep my commandments." He doesn't say, "you have to" or "you must" keep my commandments. It's simple; if we love him we will just want to.

Maybe one of the most important things to me is to have child-like faith, to rely on God no matter what. I may not always understand, but I know I must trust and have faith in God. That's the kind of faith I saw in my Mom. I always hoped that Jesus would return before anything happened to either of my parents, but my Mom passed away when she was only 68 years old. When our family was faced with her illness, and then her death, I was amazed at the peace we had, that "peace that transcends all understanding" (Philippians 4:7). Her peace with God was a blessing to us. I want to have that same simple faith.

It is so interesting to look back over time and see how things have worked out, knowing God has been there all the time, leading and guiding in our lives. I don't believe God causes bad things to happen; it's totally because we live in a sinful world. That's where we must have faith. People told me that I'd go through all kinds of stages of grief when my mom passed away, one of them being angry at God, but I was never angry with Him. God gave me strength and courage and peace to make it through such a sad time in my life, and He has given me such a beautiful hope: the hope of His return!

When our oldest daughter was diagnosed with a brain tumor in her sophomore year of high school, our lives were suddenly halted and put into fast motion at the same time. She had an MRI, doctor visits, diagnosis, a second opinion, and then surgery, all within a week. We went from wrapping up another school year to wondering whether or not she had cancer, if our girl would walk, talk, or see when the surgery was finished, or make it through at all. She was the bravest girl I have been blessed to know and love. Before surgery, a dear pastor friend prayed for her. He asked her how she was feeling and she said she had peace. She knew that, no matter what happened, Jesus would be with her; she was in His loving arms. Her childlike faith in God gave her peace. As a Mom, knowing how she felt strengthened me. I prayed for that same peace to fill my heart, and it did! Jesus saw her through the surgery and weeks of therapy and recovery, and two months later she was able to walk into school with her sister by her side for support. All is well! She had a full recovery, and is healthy and so happy.

Q: If a non-Christian were to ask you what they could do to establish and maintain a consistent Christian life, what would you suggest?

I would go back to the basics, pray! Lay everything out to Jesus; ask Him to come into your life and fill your heart. Tell Him how you're feeling. Ask Him to influence your thinking and show you the changes you should make in your life. Ask for forgiveness and for Him to give you peace and patience and a love for everyone. Take time to help others. Prayer is the key to a relationship with God. Let your relationship with Him grow as it would when spending time with a friend. Quality time is a must in order to grow any relationship. God wants us to spend time with Him. He is there for us, waiting like a kind, patient friend, our Brother, our Father. How can the almighty God of the universe of all creation, want to spend time with us? It's hard to believe, but He does. He made a way for us to spend all eternity with Him and it cost Him so dearly, but that's how I know He loves me. He is ready to send His Holy Spirit to live in us and guide us through this life, this journey to Heaven.

GUIDANCE FROM JACK:

Q: What do you do on a regular basis to maintain a consistent Christian life?

Prayer. It does not always work, of course that's my fault, however, prayer slows me down, allows me to be more aware of what I need to do, how I need to present myself and react or follow through.

Read. As with prayer, reading puts concepts/thoughts in my head that I carry with me throughout the day. It's a wonderful reflection tool. Also, don't just read the Bible, there are many good Christian authors.

Service. Serving others takes some of my selfishness away. Serving others, no matter how small, allows me to consider ways I might serve others in the future. Christ's life on this earth was a life of service.

Q: If a non-Christian were to ask you what they could do to establish and maintain a consistent Christian life, what would you suggest?

I would ask why do they want to be a Christian? It makes "becoming" a Christian theirs.

Read books from multiple authors; start with books on faith and prayer. Building a foundation would be important, we all have our thoughts on faith and becoming a Christian, reading and reflecting makes for a real foundation.

Share different books on the life of Christ. Christ equals Christianity. If we read and reflect on the life of Christ, it's very difficult not to want to put our best efforts towards reflecting his life.

Invite them to be a part of a study group, staying singular while trying to establish a Christian lifestyle would be difficult.

Ask them about service activities, do they participate? Would they like to? In service we share, and it strengthens our faith. It's not always comfortable.

GUIDANCE FROM CASEY:

Q: What do you do on a regular basis to maintain a consistent Christian life?

Write in my prayer journal daily. It keeps me focused, keeps my thoughts from wondering, reminds me of my prayer list (both those who still need prayer and answers to prayer). Reminds me to surrender my will daily and let God work His will in me.

Read both a morning and evening devotional/Bible section/"help" book. It gives me reminders for daily living, how great God is, and what God has done for me, His love in action for me, etc. For instance, we just finished our evening reading book about attitudes as compared to the children in the wilderness. A great eye-opener. My current morning book is on angel stories.

Post Bible texts/song words/encouraging words where I can see them often. It is a long day between morning and evening, and these work as great reminders of God's love for me and that He is present in my life.

Listen to Christian instrumental music at work. I find myself going over the words in my mind; it's a great reminder of God's love and care.

Go to church on a regular basis. I know this is not important for everyone, but for me, it's like recharging my batteries, getting a jump start for the coming week. I love hearing someone else's take on familiar Scripture, talking with friends I don't see anywhere else, find out situations I need to be praying for, etc.

Q: If a non-Christian were to ask you what they could do to establish and maintain a consistent Christian life, what would you suggest?

Prayer and Bible study every day. For some of us who were raised in Christian schools, it sometimes feels like we know all the Bible has to tell us. But as I spend time in prayer, I'm convinced that I have so much to learn and to change in my life. I want to stay in tune with what God has planned for me, but if I never talk to Him, read His word, how can I possibly follow that path. For a new Christian, I would suggest the gospels, those stories that make Jesus real. Having a prayer life is different for everyone. Read a book on prayer and options; find something that works.

Meet and talk with other Christians, either at church, or weekly Bible studies. Sometimes a fellow co-worker can be your encouragement. Encouragement and positive feedback is what we all need for all areas of life.

Don't get discouraged. There will be days (possibly weeks) when you don't feel like praying, or can't find time to read and study. Life gets in the way. Treat each day as a new beginning and go from there.

GUIDANCE FROM WENDY:

Q: What do you do on a regular basis to maintain a consistent Christian life?

Workbooks. These give me a guideline to follow. Sometimes I get sort of lost on what to read in the Bible, and these workbooks give me direction on what text to study. I buy my workbooks from Christian bookstores, but there are many online versions as well. I personally prefer to handwrite my notes and to have the book in hand. Making sure the workbook uses the Bible as its primary study material is important to me so that I may learn directly from the Word of God without many outside sources weaved in.

Have Scripture memorized. If I didn't know the Word of God, I think my life would be a downward spiral. There are so many lies that Satan throws at me every day: "You're not good enough" or "God doesn't love you." The Bible tells us to think on whatever is true and noble (Philippians 4:8). I find myself often having to replace lies with truths from the Bible. If I didn't have the truths, the lies would soon dwell and become things I believed about myself. I use memorized Scripture daily to defeat lies. To memorize Scripture, I write down the verse and tape it to a mirror or refrigerator so that I can see it every day. There are also online apps that I have used to challenge me with memorization.

Christian friendships/accountability. My friends point me toward truth and they are a huge source of encouragement in my walk with Christ. We get together at least monthly, but talk via phone more often. They hold me accountable for areas in my Christian faith that I need some growth. They bring me challenge. They make me better.

Podcasts and music. In this season of life, my life is super hectic. It's not always easy for me to find quiet time. Podcasts and worship music are great for me right now because I can multitask while listening. I listen to podcasts by reliable speakers/pastors. I can listen to those while I am cooking, showering, driving, or cleaning the house. The same goes with music. In a world full of a lot of discouragement it is nice to feed your heart (or ears) with as much truth whenever possible.

Q: If a non-Christian were to ask you what they could do to establish and maintain a consistent Christian life, what would you suggest?

Get involved in a small group. Community is so important in our Christian faith. You need Christian groups for constant truth and encouragement. There is also so much wisdom and potential in life-long friendships.

Find an older mentor. The Bible makes it clear that there is a lot of wisdom to be gained from our elders. I think finding an older Christian mentor to meet with weekly or monthly is a good, practical idea to keep you on track.

Step out of your comfort zone. Finding a small group and mentor is awkward if you're anything like me (shy and introverted). The initial step is weird and so uncomfortable, but nothing great really happens when you live your life comfortable. The great things that happen in our lives all involve taking risks. You're going to have to take a leap of faith and ask to join that church, or that small group, or ask someone to mentor you. Being vulnerable is anything but comfortable, but stick with it because there is so much reward that comes from it.

Establish boundaries. Only you know the things that might tempt you into getting off track with your Christian faith. In college, I avoided going to parties. I knew that going to parties wasn't sinful, but it wasn't beneficial for my personal walk with the Lord, so I avoided them. If you have a boyfriend/girlfriend, maybe you decide not to be alone together. Whatever takes from your Christian walk, establish a boundary and stick with it. It is also a great idea to share your boundaries with your new small group and mentor, because they will help hold you accountable.

Don't be afraid to let people know up front, your values/boundaries. People may not always have the same values as you, but it's okay (and encouraged) that you share your values with them as soon as possible. You'll be surprised at how well they hear you and respect your values. It will (hopefully) make the temptations easier for you. My colleagues knew that I didn't attend parties, they respected my decision and never really invited me to go with them. That helped me a lot. People will know what to expect from you.

Know the gospel and give yourself grace. I think it's important for you to learn and study the characteristics of how God loves you (the gospel). Give yourself grace because God gives you grace. I used to believe that I had to be perfect in order to be loved by God. My faith was like a roller coaster because I would sin, feel guilty, run away from God because I thought He hated me, then I would come back. After studying the gospel, I learned that there was nothing that I could do to earn God's love, and there was nothing that I have done that would make him love me any less. His love doesn't work that way. Once you know that and understand it, I think your Christian walk will be changed forever.

GUIDANCE FROM SHELLY:

Q: What do you do on a regular basis to maintain a consistent Christian life?

Pray. Praying before meals, before bed, or just randomly when I feel the need keeps me close to Jesus.

Go to church. Going to church on Sunday keeps me accountable week to week.

Lead by example. I do my best to "walk the walk" and make the best choices possible. I know that my husband depends on me, and my son and siblings look up to me. I want to be the best example for them as I can.

Study Scripture. I should turn to Scripture way more than I do, so I am guilty of not always following through with this one. I do, however, have a "life verse".

Trust in the Lord with all thy heart; and lean not unto thine own understanding. In all thy ways acknowledge him, and he shall direct thy paths (Proverbs 3:5-6).

Anytime I am feeling down or if I ever question my faith, I can turn to that verse and somehow it always picks me up.

Q: If a non-Christian were to ask you what they could do to establish and maintain a consistent Christian life, what would you suggest?

Visit churches. Finding a "home church" and going regularly is important in maintaining a Christian lifestyle. In my opinion, no matter how busy your week is, Sundays always seem to make me slow down and check in with my faith.

Pray regularly. Turning to God throughout the day, whether it is to pray for someone who is sick, or thank God for something positive in your life, is a great way to maintain a Christian life.

Read Scripture. There are so many verses in the Bible that relate to life experiences. Finding a "life verse" to live by has been helpful to me. As I mentioned earlier, anytime I am feeling down or questioning my faith, I can refer back to my life verse and somehow it picks me up. I feel like this would be helpful to others as well if they are trying to maintain a consistent Christian life.

IN CONCLUSION

*I*n this book I have relived a variety of experiences that had an impact on the direction of my life. My Christian life has been like a roller coaster ride, with many highs and lows. When I was young, the future sometimes looked bleak and hopeless. Growing up I felt so much pressure and anxiety. I was expected to live up to my parent's dogmatic expectations when I envisioned totally different goals and outcomes.

Maintaining a consistent Christian life was much more difficult when I was also rebelling against the SDA church. I have been critical of some SDA doctrines and SDA employees. I have always found some SDA methodology to be problematic. Some SDA employees have been difficult for me to accept because from my prospective they were predominantly legalistic, judgmental, and displayed little or no Christ-like attributes.

I have thought about the fact that as an administrator, teacher, and coach I was also in a position to make mistakes and cause a student or co-worker to feel the same way about me as I have certain colleagues, supervisors, and administrators. I have known who some of those were and have tried to contact them and apologize. If there are others,

I want them to know that I am sorry if I have in any way offended them.

Many of my best friends are SDA and I do not want in any way to hurt them. The experiences in this book are personal to me and certainly not meant to be a generalization of the SDA church or its people. Many great people and students I have worked with have had similar stories to tell, and they represent many different denominations and doctrines.

When I left professional baseball, I felt convinced that the Lord had more meaningful work for me to do than to pursue my own selfish goals. I spent thirty years in SDA educational endeavors believing this is where the Lord had lead me. I had many wonderful experiences with terrific young people along the way.

I made plenty of mistakes. When I did, I sometimes got a nurturing hand from a caring Christian supervisor. On the other hand, I often got the wrath of some legalistic SDA supervisors who showed no semblance of Christ-like attributes. I have asked God to come into my heart and soften my anger from those who I felt betrayed me.

I said some twenty years ago that I would never again be an SDA. I'm not so sure now that this is the case. However, I am sure that I want to have a relationship with Jesus Christ first and foremost, and let the Holy Spirit lead.

I do believe that my life could not have evolved to where it is now, without divine intervention. I praise and thank the Lord for that.

TED EVANS

ACKNOWLEDGMENTS

I would love to be able to thank personally the many people who had a positive impact on my life.

They include but are not limited to:

My mom and dad. They were both orphans, but provided us with so much. Our struggles were real but, in the end, it is so gratifying that through God's grace we were able to part ways as a loving family. One of the main decisions that they made on my behalf was not to sign for me the first time I had a chance to play professional baseball. I am so grateful now that they made that decision, for if they had signed, there is a strong possibility that I would have been drafted and deployed to Vietnam.

My brother Clyde, who set the example for me that I seldom lived up to, and for the personal guidance he gave me along the way. He was always a sweet loving brother who early in my life watched over Tim and me.

My brother Tim, who I loved dearly. We were in the same grade and loved to compete together on the same teams. When we competed against each other it could get heated, for he hated to lose as much as I did. He was the person that provided so many great memories as we were growing up.

Mr. Manley, Business Manager at PUC. He is one of the godliest men I have ever met. What an example he was of the Holy Spirit living in a human being. For some reason, from the beginning he believed in me. He helped me get into school, find a Job, helped keep me out of the Vietnam War, and was a continuous source of support.

Jerry Fessler, my college roommate. He was a pre-med student and a person who took an interest in me. Along with his mom, dad, and sisters, Sue and Jane, he made a huge impact on my life when I needed it most. He is still a close friend.

Everett Schlisner, who I met in my freshman year in college. He befriended me and we became lifelong friends. He was instrumental in helping me get several professional positions, but more importantly, as a man who modeled exceptional character, he helped shape my life.

Duane and Ron Qualley, who I have known since my junior year in high school. Duane was my roommate in college, and Ron and I worked together in the dorm at Southern College. They have been close friends to both Tim and me, and we have shared so many experiences and great times together.

Jim and Kelly Moss. Jim was the rascal the women's dean had been upset about when I first got to Thunderbird Academy in Scottsdale, Arizona. He lived with us for a year when we first moved to Collegedale, Tennessee. Jim lost his first wife Dawn to cancer, and some years later married Kelly. We have remained close to Jim and are so happy that he found such a wonderful mate in Kelly.

Reed Christman, who befriended me at Andrews and continually beat me at golf. He is a constant joy to be with. I thoroughly enjoy his company, humor, and his guiding insights. He has remained a lifelong friend. He and his wife Patty have been a great help in the finishing of this book.

Matt and John Nafie, who are like brothers to me. They have and continue to have a tremendous impact on my life. Both have been loyal friends, but more specifically they have been positive and influential Christian consultants.

Steve Jaecks, who I played ball with and worked with for almost forty years. He worked tirelessly as my assistant coach for both the McKee men's softball team and the Gym-Masters. We were so close that around campus seldom did anyone say his name without saying mine. It was always Jaecks and Evans. He is the epitome of the perfect friend.

Suzy Evans, my wonderful wife. I have often thanked the Lord for his leading when I was not allowed to return to MBA for my senior year in high school. If I had returned to MBA, I probably would never have met Suzy. She has been the most important and influential person in my life for over fifty years. She is the most wonderful woman I have ever met. She gave me the confidence to go on with my life independently . She is the calming influence when I need it, which is all the time. She has put up with my extreme Type A personality and remained the most loyal and supportive wife. People always ask me if she is as nice at home as she is at work, and I always say; absolutely not. That is when she takes all of her pent-up frustration out on me. However, the truth of the matter is, she is just a naturally sweet person, loves people, and thank the Lord she loves me. She is the love of my life.

www.ingramcontent.com/pod-product-compliance
Lightning Source LLC
Chambersburg PA
CBHW051726040426
42447CB00008B/997